SINGAPORE ARCHITECTURE

A SHORT HISTORY

PERIPLUS

Published in 2004 by Periplus Editions (HK) Ltd.,
with editorial offices at 130 Joo Seng Road, #06-01/03, Singapore 368357
by arrangement with Pesaro Publishing, Sydney, Australia.

ISBN 0-7946-0232-0

Editor: Patrick Bingham-Hall
Design: Felicity Hayward

Photography © 2004 Patrick Bingham-Hall
Text: © 2004 Robert Powell and Pesaro Publishing

All rights reserved. No part of this publication may be reproduced, stored
in or introduced into a retrieval system or transmitted in any form or by any
means, electronic or otherwise, without the prior permission of the
publishers.

Distributed by:

North America, Latin America & Europe
Tuttle Publishing
364 Innovation Drive, North Clarendon, VT 05759-9436
Tel: (802) 773 8930 Fax: (802) 773 6993
Email: info@tuttlepublishing.com

Japan
Tuttle Publishing
Yaekari Building, 3rd Floor
5-4-12 Osaki, Shinagawa-ku, Tokyo 141-0032
Fax: (03) 5437 0171 Fax: (03) 5437 0755
Email: tuttle-sales@gol.com

Asia-Pacific
Berkeley Books Pte. Ltd.
130 Joo Seng Road, #06-01/03, Singapore 368357
Tel. (65) 6280 1330 Fax: (65) 6280 6290
Email: inquiries@periplus.com.sg

Colour Origination by Universal Graphics, Singapore
Printed and Bound by Star Standard Industries, Singapore

SINGAPORE ARCHITECTURE

ROBERT POWELL

Photographs by Patrick Bingham-Hall

PERIPLUS

CONTENTS //

PAGE 8

1819 – 1867
THE EAST INDIA COMPANY – THE FOUNDATIONS OF MODERN SINGAPORE

12 South Boat Quay 1822
13 Kampong Glam 1822
14 Chinatown 1822
15 Fuk Tak Ch'i Temple 1824
16 Old Parliament House 1826 – 1827
17 Nagore Durgha Indian Muslim Shrine 1828 – 1830
18 Old Christian Cemetery, Fort Canning 1834
19 Armenian Church 1835
20 Jamae (Chulia) Mosque 1830 – 1835
21 The Istana Kampong Glam 1840
22 Thian Hock Keng Temple 1839 – 1842
24 Sri Mariamman Temple 1843
25 Little India 1844
26 Hajjah Fatimah Mosque 1846
27 Cathedral of the Good Shepherd 1843 – 1846
28 State of Johore Mosque 1849
29 Convent of the Holy Infant Jesus 1854
30 Fort Canning 1859
31 Botanic Gardens and Burkill Hall 1859
32 Victoria Memorial Hall and Theatre 1856 – 1862
33 St Andrews Cathedral 1856 – 1862
34 St Josephs Institute 1865 – 1867
35 Empress Place Building 1864 – 1867

PAGE 36

1867 – 1918
A CROWN COLONY – THE CROSSROADS OF SOUTHEAST ASIA

38 The Istana 1867 – 1869
39 Cavanagh Bridge 1868 – 1869
40 Tan Si Chong Su Temple 1876
41 Orchard Road Presbyterian Church 1877 – 1878
42 Sun Yat Sen Villa 1880
43 Singapore Cricket Club 1884
44 Tan Yeok Nee House 1885
45 Raffles Hotel 1886
46 National Museum 1886 – 1887
47 Thong Chai Medical Hall 1892
48 Telok Ayer Market 1894
49 Atbara 1898
50 Goodwood Park Hotel 1900
52 Emerald Hill Road 1901
53 Jinriksha Building 1903
54 Eden Hall - British High Commissioner's Residence 1904
55 Chesed-El Synagogue 1905
56 Central Fire Station 1909
57 Tao Nan School 1910
58 St George's Church, Tanglin 1911
59 Madrasah Alsagoff 1912

PAGE 60

918–1942
THE TWILIGHT OF THE BRITISH EMPIRE

62 Goodwood Hill 1920s
63 The College of Medicine Building
    (Ministry of Health) 1923–1926
64 Great Southern Hotel 1927
65 Sultan Mosque 1924–1928
66 The Fullerton Building – The General
    Post Office 1919–1928
67 City Hall 1926–1929
68 Koon Seng Road 1929
69 Capital Building 1929–1930
70 31 and 33 Club Street 1932
71 Clifford Pier 1931–1933
72 23 Ridout Road 1934
73 Hill Street Building 1934–1936
74 Kallang Airport 1937
76 Singapore Railway Station 1932–1937
77 Chee Guan Chiang House 1938
78 The Supreme Court 1937–1939
79 WWII Pillbox 1942

PAGE 80

1942–1975
THE BIRTH OF A NATION: AN INDEPENDENT SINGAPORE

84 Nassim Hill Apartments 1950–1951
85 Tiong Bahru Housing Estate
    1936–1954
86 Asia Insurance Building 1954
87 Bank of China Building 1953–1954
88 Blessed Sacrament Church
    1961–1963
89 Peoples Park Complex 1970–1973
90 Jurong Town Hall 1970
92 Golden Mile Complex 1974
93 OCBC Tower 1975
94 Futura Apartments 1973–1976
95 Pearl Bank Apartments 1976
96 Singapore Power Building 1971–1977
97 Pandan Valley Condominium
    1973–1979
98 Regent Hotel 1983
99 Unit 8 1983
100 The Colonnade 1985
101 Parkway Centre 1985
102 Raffles City 1984–85
103 Habitat Ardmore Park 1984–1986
104 Tampines North Community
    Centre 1989
105 Singapore Indoor Stadium 1990

PAGE 106

1991–2003
ARCHITECTURE AND THE GLOBAL CITY

110 Hitachi Tower / Caltex House 1993
111 Eu House I 1993–1994
112 The Concourse 1994
113 King Albert Park House 1992–1994
114 Tampines New Town 1994
115 Wheelock Place 1994
116 UOB Plaza 1993–1995
117 Temasek Polytyechnic 1995
118 Eastpoint Shopping Centre 1996
119 Millenia Tower 1996
120 Check House I 1996
121 Genesis 1994–1997
122 Nassim Jade 1997
123 Windsor Park House 1997
124 Kadang Kerbau Hospital 1988–1997
125 Institute of Southeast Asian
    Studies 1998
126 Morley Road House 1998
127 Camden Medical Centre 1999
128 Coronation Road West House
    1998–2000
129 The Gallery Hotel 2000
130 Victoria Park Houses 2000
131 Marine Parade Community
    Centre 2000
132 Expo MRT Station 2001
133 Trevose Crescent 2002
134 The Esplanade – Theatres on the
    Bay 1994–2002
135 Tree House 2002
136 1 Moulmein Rise 2003
137 Lincoln Modern 2003
138 The Arris 2003
139 Villa-O 2003

140 Maps
142 Index
144 Footnotes

A SHORT HISTORY OF SINGAPORE ARCHITECTURE
// ROBERT POWELL

The origins of Singapore are clouded in myth and conjecture. It may have been the 2nd Century 'Sabara' of Ptolemy's Golden Khersonese or the 'P'u Luo Chung' (island at the end of the peninsula) referred to by K'ang T'ai, a Chinese explorer in 231 AD.[1] Arab sailors mention the port of Ma'it, which existed in the 9th Century, and the Venetian traveller Marco Polo wrote of the settlement of Chiamassie. Both may have been referring to Singapore. Less circumstantial evidence suggests that a settlement of Temasek (Singapura in Sanskrit) came into existence in the 13th Century. According to Malay annals (Sejarah Melayu) Raja Chulan, a South Indian King, married a local princess, and their son Sang Nila Utama (who took the title Sri Tri Buana) became ruler of the Indianised Sri Vijaya Empire, based in Sumatra. In 1297 or 1299 Sri Tri Buana landed on the island and gave it the name Singapura (Lion City). He built a palace on the hill overlooking the river. The hill was protected by an earth wall, 5 metres wide at the base and 3 metres high.

The settlement prospered as a port, and in the process attracted the attention and envy of the Hindu empire of Majapahit, based in Java. The settlement is referred to in the Javanese Nagarakretagama (1365) using the old name Temasek. In 1376 the Majapahits raided Singapura, though there are conflicting views on whether this was for the purpose of occupying the island or merely to plunder.[2] Although no physical structures survived, gold jewellery dating from the period was unearthed in 1928 during excavation for a reservoir on Fort Canning Hill.

In 1390 Iskander, also known as Parameswara, a Sailendra Prince of Palembang, renounced his allegiance to Majapahit and arrived in Singapura. In due course he orchestrated the assassination of the local chief who owed loyalty to Siam, but in fear of retribution from the rising state of Ayuthaya he decamped to Malacca in 1402–1403. Some sources say he was driven out by the Raja of Pahang.[3] With his departure, the settlement of Singapura went into a steady decline and became a refuge for pirates. In 1613 the Portuguese reportedly burned down a Malay outpost at the mouth of the river. Thereafter little is known of the island but Captain Alexander Hamilton referred to it in an account of a voyage from England to China via Johore in 1703.[4]

The island eventually became part of the Johore sultanate, and in the early years of the 19th Century a kampong was re-established on the former site of Singapura by Temanggong Abdul Rahman, who was beholden to his elder brother Sultan Hussein Mahomed Shah, Sultan of Johore.

Here is all life and activity: and it would be difficult to name a place on the globe with brighter prospects or more present satisfaction

SIR STAMFORD RAFFLES July 1819

1819 – 1867 // THE EAST INDIA COMPANY – THE FOUNDATIONS OF MODERN SINGAPORE

An English East India Company flotilla of eight ships, commanded by Sir Stamford Raffles, dropped anchor off St John's Island at the mouth of the Singapore River on 28th January 1819. The settlement of Singapore at the time consisted of a substantial wood and *atap* house occupied by Temanggong Abdul Rahman, surrounded by a few huts occupied by the 20 or 30 members of his entourage and a large number of boats clustered on the river.[5]

There were perhaps a thousand inhabitants in Singapore in 1819, including 20 or 30 Chinese settlers who lived on plantations about five kilometres up-river, and 500 Orang Kallang, 200 Orang Seletar, 150 Orang Gelam and other Orang Laut or sea nomads.

Two days after arriving at the river mouth, Raffles (at that time Lieutenant Governor of Bencoolen) signed a preliminary treaty with the Temanggong to set up an East India Company 'factory' or trading post. The site seemed ideal, for the ground on the north-east bank of the river was level and firm. There was a good supply of drinking water and the river mouth formed a natural harbour. The location, at the southernmost tip of the Asian mainland, commanded the approach to the Straits of Malacca and was conveniently sited to trade with China and the Indonesian archipelago.

Having set up the trading post, Raffles departed, leaving Colonel William Farquhar as Resident. When Raffles returned on 31st May 1819, bringing new immigrants and building materials from Malacca, he was delighted with the progress being made. On this occasion he established a conceptual plan for the town, which for purposes of order and control grouped the different communities in specific areas.

Raffles left Singapore for a second time on 25th June 1819, and did not return for three years. In that time, under Farquhar, the settlement grew at a spectacular rate. In the first two and a half years 3,000 vessels called at Singapore. The possibility of making a new life and of profitable employment attracted migrants from all over Asia and Europe. The foundations of modern Singapore as a global trading hub were established. By 1821 there were 5,000 inhabitants, which included 3,000 Malays, more than 1,000 Chinese and 500 Bugis together with Indians, Arabs, Armenians, Europeans, Eurasians and numerous other minority groups.[6]

But when Raffles returned to Singapore on 10th October 1822 he was furious to find that Colonel Farquhar had, against his instructions, permitted the European merchants to build their *godowns* (warehouses) on the south and north banks of the river. The latter intruded into the area Raffles had allotted for Government buildings. He immediately called upon Farquhar to resign, and appointed a committee to replan the south side of the river. After consulting with George Drumgold Coleman[7], an architect at that time in practice in Batavia, he gave instructions for the reclamation of what would become known as South Boat Quay. It developed as "a picturesque townscape along the curve of the River that has been compared with the Regent Quadrant of London of the time".[8]

In a memorandum to the Town committee on 4th November 1822, Raffles outlined the manner in which Singapore was to be developed. John Nash's plan for Regent Street in London (1812, constructed from 1817 to 1823) was contemporary with the plan for Singapore and it probably influenced Raffles in that it demonstrated the effective control of the planning of a city.[9]

The emergence of the shophouse as the dominant urban typology in Singapore was possibly due to Raffles having been Lieutenant Governor presiding over British interests in Java between 1811 and 1816. He would have observed that the narrow warehouses of the Dutch East India Company were fronted by verandahs. The shophouse was a hybrid of the narrow fronted house of Amsterdam and the courtyard houses of southern China. But Raffles was also familiar with the regular layout of the 'native lines' in India. His memorandum therefore called for an orthogonal planning grid, with continuous walkways (known as 'five-foot ways') to join the commercial premises and facilitate the movement of pedestrians during inclement weather.

Shophouses – Tanjong Pagar Road

Land to the south-west of the Singapore River, beyond the warehouses of the European merchants, was allotted for the Chinese community. The directive separated the Chinese according to the "provincial and other distinctions".[10] Thus Hokkiens subsequently occupied Telok Ayer Street, China Street and Chulia Street; Teochew-speaking Chinese were directed to Circular Road, Boat Quay and South Bridge Road; and the Cantonese occupied mainly Kreta Ayer, Upper Cross Street, New Bridge Road, Bukit Pasoh and parts of South Bridge Road.[11] Chulia Indians were allocated land upriver from the Chinese.

The same directive allocated land to the European Town, to the Sultan's descendants and to the Bugis and the Arabs. The directive noted that Malays "being principally attached to the Tumongong (sic), or engaged in fishing, may not require any very extensive allotment".[12] In 1820 five hundred Bugis settlers, including wives and children, arrived from the Riau islands and were allocated land on the Rochor River.

Raffles was familiar with the Indian *Maidan* and provided for an open square that would become the Padang (open field) fronting the church and the courthouse. A Commercial Square was also planned on the south side of the river. Lieutenant Philip Jackson (1802-1870) drew up a Master Plan for the development of the town in 1823, and each race began to place its imprint on the landscape in the form of churches, shrines, mosques, temples, humble dwellings, official residences, warehouses and government buildings.

Although the ethnic concentration of Chinese in Chinatown and Malays in Kampong Glam was subsequently diluted by Government housing policies from 1965 onwards, both areas to this day retain a strong sense of ethnic identity.

THE COLEMAN LEGACY

Born in Drogheda in Ireland, GD Coleman (1796-1844) was Singapore's first architect with any formal training. He was in practice in Batavia from 1820 but settled in Singapore in 1826, and was appointed Surveyor of Lands in succession to Lieutenant Philip Jackson. In 1833 he was appointed Superintendent of Public Works and (Indian) Convicts. He was to remain in the post until 1841. He was responsible for the design of a private house in High Street (the first road constructed in the settlement) for a prominent merchant John Argyle Maxwell (1826 – 1827). The house was never occupied by Maxwell and upon completion was rented to the East India Company to serve as the settlement's court house. Later the house became the Legislative Assembly Building and from 1965 to 1997 served as Parliament House. The Palladian-style house was subsequently modified and extended on several occasions, but some fragments of the original building remain.

Coleman's finest work was the Armenian Church of St. Gregory The Illuminator (1835), an elegant symmetrical Palladian building. He also designed H C Caldwell's House (1840), which was located in the grounds of the Convent of the Holy Infant Jesus. It is thought Coleman was also responsible for the Istana Kampong Glam (1840) built for Sultan Ali Iskander Shah, the son of Sultan Hussein, who together with Temenggong Abdul Rahman signed the 1819 treaty with the East India Company.

Coleman died in 1844 and was buried at the cemetery on Government Hill. Today, all that remains of the cemetery are the Gothic gateways, built in 1846, two small Classical monuments and several tombstones.

In the wake of Coleman came John Turnbull Thomson, who was appointed Government Surveyor (1841–1853). J T Thomson's main responsibility was land survey, but he also became involved in several buildings. Most of these buildings, such as the Ellenborough Building (1845) and the original Tan Tock Seng Hospital (1844) have not survived, but one that is thought to be to his design is the Hajjah Fatimah Mosque (1845–1846).

Dennis Lesley McSwinney arrived in Singapore in 1836 and was employed as clerk to GD Coleman. McSwinney designed the Cathedral of the Good Shepherd (1843–1846), a Palladian style building with round arches, tall columns and a generous entrance porch. A tower and spire, designed by Charles Alexander Dyce, were added one year later in 1847. These were the principal architects (the word is used in its broadest sense, since not all were trained professionals) who operated in Singapore from 1822 to 1853. They all wore several hats, sometimes undertaking private commissions in addition to their official appointments.

The State of Johore Mosque (1849) in Telok Blangah Road shows evidence of GD Coleman's influence and was probably designed by one of the architects who followed immediately after him. The influence of Coleman on the development of architecture in Singapore was profound.[13] He set the trend for architectural design, and the Palladian theme he used can be seen in St Andrews Church and the Armenian Church. Other architects who followed continued in this style. The granting of firm land leases at this time encouraged more substantial buildings.

Not only did Coleman introduce European Palladian elements into Singapore's architecture, but his advice on urban planning was crucial for he was familiar with Renaissance town planning and the layout of both European cities and Calcutta, the capital of British India.

A MIGRANT COMMUNITY

The Islamic religion was conveyed to Southeast Asia by Indian Muslim merchants from India, by Arabs via Sumatra and Java, and from Arabia itself, and was established long before Raffles set up the Singapore trading post. But the arrival of substantial numbers of Indian and Arab migrants in Singapore following the initial success of the East India Company factory caused several mosques and shrines to be built. These included the Nagore Durgha Indian Muslim Shrine (1828–1830) built by South Indian Muslims who arrived in Singapore from the Coromandel Coast, and the Jamae (Chulia) Mosque (1830-1835) in South Bridge Road, also built by Chulia Indians, on the site of an earlier brick structure begun in 1826.

The rapid expansion of the port activities under the auspices of the East India Company attracted a flood of migrants from China, and they too erected religious buildings. They were often erected at the point of landfall as tokens of thanksgiving for a safe voyage. The Fuk Tak Ch'i Temple (1824) in Telok Ayer Street was erected on the site of an earlier wood and *atap* building erected in 1820 on the shoreline facing the ocean.

Another temple on Telok Ayer Street is the Thian Hock Keng Temple (1839–1842). It was erected on the site of a joss house dedicated to Ma-Chu-Po, the Goddess of the Sea, where newly arrived immigrants from Fukien Province in China gave thanks for their safe voyage. Anonymous designers who followed traditional themes built these and other early temples. They were direct importations from South China, and were largely composite variations of Buddhist, Taoist and Confucian elements.[14]

Local Indian and Chinese artisans similarly built Hindu temples, although their (anonymous) designers, sculptors and artists were usually brought from India. They follow closely the forms of Tamil temples of South India. The oldest Hindu temple is the Sri Mariamman Temple (1843) in South Bridge Road, built on the site of a timber structure erected in 1827 by Nariana Pillay, who journeyed to Singapore from Penang on Raffles' flagship, the Indiana.

From the 1840s onwards, an area at the south end of Serangoon Road became the focus of Indian migrants. It includes Buffalo Road and Kerbau Road and is referred to as Little India. It is the location of other Hindu Temples including the Sri Srinivasa Perumal Temple (1855, rebuilt 1961–1966) built on land bought from the East India Company.

SOLDIERS AND PRIESTS

The mid-1840s saw the retirement or death of the initial group of architects and surveyors, and there was an influx of new designers. Several were army officers. Captain CEF Faber of the Madras Engineers arrived in 1844 and was appointed Superintendent

Engineer. Colonel Ronald MacPherson of the Madras Artillery arrived in 1855 and was appointed Executive Engineer and Superintendent of Convicts. He was superseded by Captain (later Major) JFA McNair, also of the Madras Artillery who arrived in Singapore in 1856.

In 1858 the East India Company was abolished following the Indian Mutiny of May 10th 1857. Singapore passed directly under the control of the British Government's India Office in Calcutta, and Colonel George Collyer was appointed Chief Engineer, a position he held until 1862. John Bennett, a Civil and Mechanical Engineer, also arrived in Singapore in 1854.

Perhaps the shock of the Indian Mutiny in May 1857 awakened the realisation that Singapore was somewhat lightly defended from insurrection or attack from outside. Whatever the reason, in 1857 the military acquired Government Hill and erected fortifications including seven 68-pound guns, and two years later the hill was renamed Fort Canning after Viscount George Canning, Governor-General of India (1857–1862). The Fort was never used in hostilities and was eventually demolished in 1907, but a gateway and part of the original fortifications survived and were restored in 1993.

There was also an influx of priest-architects. The French Catholic priest Father Beurel arrived in Singapore in 1836 with the intention of starting schools for girls and boys of all races and religions.[15] In 1852 he brought out six Catholic brothers including Louis Antoine Combes (Brother Lothaire) who was responsible for designing the centre block of St Joseph's Institute (1865–1867), a Roman Catholic boys school founded in 1852. Other priests with a talent for architecture were Father Pierre Paris and Father R P Ch Nain.

In 1854, St Andrews Cathedral church, designed by J T Thomson in 1842 (itself a replacement of an even earlier church by GD Coleman), was considered unsafe and was demolished. Colonel Ronald MacPherson designed the 1856 replacement, in the Gothic/Early English style of the 12th Century, inspired by the Gothic revival that was under way in England at the time. The English architect AWN Pugin advocated a direct reference to the spiritual values and forms of the Middle Ages. His writing after 1836 profoundly affected English buildings in the 19th Century, and influenced John Ruskin who published *The Stones of Venice* in 1853.[16] St. Andrews was built with Indian convict labour supervised by Major JFA McNair and John Bennett. It was consecrated in 1862 and the spire was added two years later.

The nearby Convent of the Holy Infant Jesus incorporates a number of excellent buildings. That the Gothic revival was persistent is evident in the Chapel that was built in the grounds in 1890, at the same time that William Morris's influential writings were in circulation in England. The Chapel was the work of Father R P Ch Nain in association with Swan and Lermit, a firm of Engineers and Surveyors, who developed the plans for submission and supervised construction. Father Nain was also the architect of the neo-Gothic Our Lady of Lourdes Church (1888) and the distinctive curved wings of the St Joseph's Institute (1906).

Meanwhile the consolidation of the Government enclave around the Padang continued with the Singapore Town Hall (1856–1862), designed by John Bennett of the Chief Engineers Office. In 1905, when the Memorial Hall and Clock Tower were added it was adapted and renamed the Victoria Memorial Hall and Theatre. The name was changed again in 1979.

The Empress Place Building (1864–1867) was originally intended to be the Government Court House, but it was to house the Chamber of the Straits Legislative Council and later still, the Immigration Department and the Singapore Registry of Citizenship. The central block was designed by Major JFA McNair, the Executive Engineer and Superintendent of Public Works.

There were relatively few women in the early years of the settlement, and the social activity of the young men employed by the merchant trading companies revolved around sport. Cricket was played on the Padang as early as 1837, and the Singapore Cricket Club (SCC) was founded in 1852. The SCC pavilion was rebuilt several times thereafter, but the 1884 building by Swan and Maclaren forms the core of the existing clubhouse.

Out of the town centre, land for the establishment of the Botanic Gardens was allocated in 1859, although the grounds were not formally opened until 1874. Burkill Hall (1866) was built in the Gardens to house the Director. It was from here that in 1888 Henry Nicholas Ridley pioneered the rubber industry in Malaya and devised a method of tapping the trees.

1822

South Boat Quay

When Sir Stamford Raffles returned for his third and final visit to the East India Company outpost in October 1822, he ordered the levelling of a hill (Mount Wallace) and the earth was used to reclaim the swampy south bank of the river. The resulting land, subsequently known as South Boat Quay was then divided into plots and allotted to merchants. By the 1860s, three-quarters of Singapore's business was transacted from *godowns* along the Boat Quay. But from 1983 onwards the area declined as business moved to the mechanised container port at Tanjong Pagar. The Boat Quay was gazetted for conservation in July 1989, and in 1994 the Urban Renewal Authority carried out upgrading of the Boat Quay infrastructure.

1822

Kampong Glam

Kampong Glam was a small village at the mouth of the Rochor River at the time of Raffles' landing in 1819. It derived its name from the *Gelam* tree that grew in the area. In 1822 Raffles drew up a master plan for Singapore, and in his recommendations to the Town Committee he assigned specific areas to the different races. Kampong Glam was allocated to Sultan Hussein Shah and his descendants, and a Malay community grew around the Sultan's compound. There has always been a large Arab presence in the area, and street names such as Baghdad Street and Muscat Street testify to this. Bussorah Street, Arab Street and the Sultan Mosque define the core area of Kampong Glam.

1822

Chinatown

Chinatown was laid out according to instructions issued by Sir Stamford Raffles to the Town Planning Committee in November 1822. An orthogonal planning grid was employed to the south of the Singapore River, with two and three-storey shophouses fronted by continuous verandahs, which were known as 'five-foot ways'. The shophouse plans probably originated from the *godowns* used by the Dutch in the port of Bencoolen, and they were a hybrid of the row houses of Amsterdam combined with the domestic buildings of Southern China. The plans were narrow and deep; the deeper houses employing at least one and often two lightwells to provide daylight and ventilation. The façades were decorated in an eclectic combination of European, Chinese and Malay elements.

1824

Fuk Tak Ch'i Temple

Far East Square

Fuk Tak Ch'i Temple (Temple of Prosperity and Virtue) dating from 1824, was the first temple built in Singapore. It belonged to the Shenist sect, which combines Buddhism and Confucianism. This brick temple was built on the site where an earlier one, erected in 1820, had stood facing the sea, and has doors painted with protective door gods. Its benefactors included Cantonese and Hakka, and its main deity is Tua Peh Kong (Dai Bak Gong in Cantonese). The temple is quite small with one internal court. It is now part of the Far East Square development, completed in 2000, which combines newly built offices and a shophouse conservation project. The temple has been adapted to form a museum featuring Chinese history and culture.

1826–1827

Old Parliament House

High Street / Empress Place

Architect // GD Coleman

Alterations and additions by THH Hancock (Public Works Department)

Originally designed as a private house for a merchant, John Argyle Maxwell. Before he could take residence it was acquired for use as a courthouse, a purpose it served until 1839. The oldest government building on the island, it was later used as offices and was extended and remodelled for its changing functions in 1875, 1901 and 1909 by the Public Works Department. In 1954 the neo-Classical building became the Legislative Assembly Building. It served as Parliament House for the elected Government of Singapore from 1965, until replaced by the New Parliament House (designed by PWD Consultants Pte Ltd) built on an adjoining site in 1999.

HISTORICAL PHOTOGRAPH COURTESY OF SINGAPORE ARCHIVES

1828–1830

Nagore Durgha Indian Muslim Shrine

140 Telok Ayer Street

This shrine, originally known as Shahul Hamid Durgha, was build by South Indian Muslims who arrived in Singapore from the Coromandel Coast. The land on which the shrine is built was granted in 1827 to one Kadarpillai on a 999-year lease, on condition that it should not be used for a temporary wood or *atap* structure. The building occupies a corner site and is a blend of Classical motifs and Indian details. Arches spring from fluted Corinthian columns, and perforated grille work adorns the upper parts of the façade. The shrine is also known as Masjid Chulia. In 2003 it was in a dilapidated state and inaccessible to the public.

1834

Old Christian Cemetery
Fort Canning

Sir Stamford Raffles erected a timber and *atap* house on the summit of Government Hill in 1823. It served as the Government Residence until 1857 when it was demolished prior to the building of Fort Canning, named after Viscount Canning, Governor General of India from 1856 to 1862. Raffles established a Christian cemetery near his house but it was moved further down the hill in 1834, and consecrated by the Bishop of Calcutta in the same year. Today, all that remains are the Gothic gateways, built in 1846, two small Classical monuments and several tombstones. In close proximity is the Keramat (shrine) of Iskander Shah.

1835

Armenian Church

Armenian Street / Hill Street

Architect // GD Coleman

By 1821, two years after Raffles established the East India Company's presence on the Singapore River, a small community of Armenians gathered regularly for religious services, and in 1827 their first priest, the Reverend Gregory Johannes, arrived. Soon after, the Armenian Church, dedicated to St. Gregory the Illuminator was erected. The delightful little church, the oldest in Singapore, was designed by the Superintendent of Public Works, George Drumgoole Coleman (1796–1844), and is an elegant symmetrical Classical building with projecting square porticos and a semi-circular chancel and altar. An English architect named Maddock added the tower and spire in 1847.

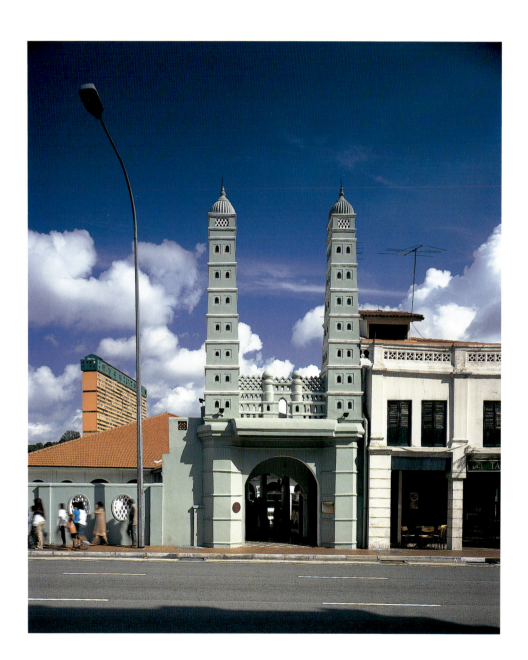

1830–1835

Jamai (Chulia) Mosque

218 South Bridge Road

Following the establishment of the East India Company trading post, there was an influx of Indian immigrants from the Coromandel Coast. The Jamai Mosque was built by these Chulia Indians on the site of an earlier brick structure begun in 1826. The principal façade, facing South Bridge Road, has twin towers with horizontal mouldings and tiny twin niches, and topped by small domes. The prayer hall is located within a surprisingly spacious inner courtyard. The architecture is an eclectic mix of Anglo-Indian, Malay and Chinese. The building was gazetted as a National Monument on 19th November 1974.

1840

Istana Kampong Glam
Sultan Gate

Architect // GD Coleman

This Palladian style Istana was built on the site of a former timber and *atap* 'palace', for Sultan Ali Iskander Shah, the son of Sultan Hussein who together with Temenggong Abdul Rahman surrendered sovereignty over the island to the East India Company. The Treaty of 1824 recognised an earlier agreement for Kampong Glam to remain in the Sultan's family so long as they lived there, though this was repealed in 1897. In the latter part of the 20th Century, the Istana, which is thought to be the design of GD Coleman, fell into a state of sad neglect. Plans to restore it were mired in sensitive issues of ownership, but by 2003 conservation work had commenced.

HISTORICAL PHOTOGRAPH COURTESY OF SINGAPORE ARCHIVES

1839–1842

Thian Hock Keng Temple

158 Telok Ayer Street

Repairs and restoration by Architects Team 3 1975–1979 and by James Ferrie and Partners 2001–2002

This is the oldest Chinese Temple in Singapore, and the most important Hokkien Buddhist place of worship. It was erected on the site of a joss house dedicated to Ma Chu-Po, the Goddess of Seafarers, where newly arrived immigrants from Fukien Province in China gave thanks for their safe voyage. Telok Ayer Street ran along the foreshore before land reclamation works in the 1880s. The temple has an elaborately decorated roof and intricately carved granite columns. It was gazetted as a National Monument on 28th June 1973, and in 1975 it was extensively restored by the Hokkien Hui Guan, the owners of the temple. James Ferrie and Partners carried out further conservation work in 2001.

1843

Sri Mariamman Temple

244 South Bridge Road

Singapore's oldest Hindu place of worship, the Sri Mariamman Temple was built on the site of a timber and *atap* structure dating from 1827. The land on which the temple stands was originally granted, in 1823, to Naraina Pillai who accompanied Sir Stamford Raffles from Penang in 1819, on Raffles' second excursion to the island. The design of the original building was executed by craftsmen from India, and it has been been rebuilt, extended and redecorated several times. It has a colourful *gopuram* and images of the cow, a sacred animal in the Hindu religion, figure prominently.

1844

Little India

Little India, unlike Chinatown and Kampong Glam, was not part of Raffles' planned settlement. It did not appear on a Town Plan of 1828, however a track was indicated as a 'Road leading across the Island' that would later become Serangoon Road. Little India refers to an area at the south end of Serangoon Road. It includes Buffalo Road and Kerbau Road in addition to many streets that still bear the names of the European houses once located here, namely Cuff Street, Norris Street and Dickson Road. The colourful and lively area was gazetted in July 1998, and numerous shophouses have subsequently been conserved.

1846

Hajjah Fatimah Mosque
Beach Road

Architect // possibly JT Thomson

Reconstructed by Chung and Wong in 1930–1932

This is the only mosque in Singapore named after a female benefactor. Hajjah Fatimah was a Malaccan lady married to a Bugis Merchant (reputedly the Sultan of Gowa in the Celebes). Her daughter Rajah Siti married Syed Ahmad of the prominent Alsagoff family, who hailed from Hadramaut, now the Peoples Republic of the Yemen. All three are buried in the private grounds of the mosque. The design juxtaposes European Classical elements, including Doric columns, alongside Chinese details. It also has a single Malaccan-style minaret and an Arab-style dome. The building was gazetted as a National Monument on 28th June 1973.

1843–1846

Cathedral of the Good Shepherd
Queen Street

Architect // Dennis Lesley McSwiney
Tower and spire by Charles Alexander Dyce 1847

D L McSwiney, a former clerk to GD Coleman, designed the Church of the Good Shepherd. The Renaissance style building has round arches, tall columns and a generous porch, and is built in the Palladian manner that he probably acquired from Coleman. The handsome cool interior has a high timber ceiling with excellent acoustics. The tower and spire, designed by CA Dyce, were added one year after the completion of the main building. The Bishop of Malacca consecrated it as the Roman Catholic Cathedral on 14th February 1897. In 1888 the nave was extended by three bays at the west end. Father Jean Marie Beurel designed the extension.

1849

State of Johore Mosque

Telok Blangah Road

This mosque is significant as the ruler of Singapore in 1819, Temenggong Abdul Rahman, lies buried here, along with his nephew Ibrahim and close relatives. Abdul Rahman was the person, together with Sultan Hussein Mahomed Shah, with whom Sir Stamford Raffles negotiated the deal whereby the East India Company initially acquired a strip of land for use as a factory. Occupying the site, along with the mosque, are a shrine known as Tanah Kubor Raja and the cemetery. The name of the architect is unknown. There is speculation that it may have been GD Coleman, or possibly one of the architects who followed immediately after him, for the design carries some features of Coleman's work.

1854

Convent of the Holy Infant Jesus

renamed CHIJMES in 1996

Victoria Street/North Bridge Road

Architect // Father RP Ch Nain and Swan & Maclaren

Alterations and additions by Ong and Ong Architects Pte Ltd and Didier Repellin 1996

The Convent of the Holy Infant Jesus occupied a whole city block, and incorporated a number of fine buildings including Caldwell's House, built 1840 and designed by GD Coleman; the Gothic inspired Chapel, designed by Father Nain, and Swan and Maclaren in 1890; St Nicholas Girls School, designed by Swan and Maclaren in 1913; and further extensions in 1951. After the school moved to new premises in 1983 the Convent fell into a state of neglect, and the Chapel was severely affected by work on underground MRT lines in the 1980s. It was the subject of an architectural competition, and in 1996 emerged as CHIJMES, a dining and entertainment complex that has managed to retain some of its charm though little of its former meaning.

1859

Fort Canning

Canning Rise / Fort Canning Road

In 1857 the military acquired Government Hill, and erected fortifications including seven 68-pound guns. In 1859 the hill was renamed Fort Canning after Viscount George Canning, Governor-General of India (1857–1862). The Fort was never used in hostilities and was demolished in 1907, but a gateway and part of the original fortifications were restored in 1993.

14th Century gold jewellery dating from the Majapahit period was unearthed in 1928 during excavation for a reservoir and a barrack block alongside the fort. In World War II, during the days that preceded the British surrender to the Japanese invasion force, Lieutenant-General Percival located his headquarters in underground bunkers at Fort Canning.

1859

Botanic Gardens and Burkill Hall

The site for the Botanic Gardens was allocated in 1859, although the gardens were not formally opened until 1874. The first rubber plants, imported from Kew Gardens in England, were planted here in 1877 and Henry Nicholas Ridley (Director of the Gardens from 1888–1912) pioneered the rubber industry in Malaya. Burkill Hall was built in 1866, and served as the residence of several of the directors of the garden, including H M Burkill (1957–1969), from whom the house takes its name. The house was constructed in a simple, graceful style with a high-hipped roof with a short ridge, deep overhanging eaves and living spaces with lofty ceilings. There are two wide verandahs on the second-storey level at the front and rear of the house.

1856–1862

Victoria Theatre and Concert Hall
Empress Place

Architect // John Bennett
Chief Engineers Office

Alterations and additions Swan and Maclaren 1905 and 1958 and by the Public Works Department 1955 and 1980

The oldest part of this building, designed by John Bennett of the Chief Engineers Office, was erected between 1856 and 1862, and initially functioned as the Singapore Town Hall. In 1905 the Memorial Hall and Clock Tower, designed by R A J Bidwell of Swan and Maclaren, were added and the Town Hall was converted to a theatre. The Peoples Action Party, which has governed Singapore since independence, was formed in an inaugural meeting held in the Memorial Hall in November 1954. The theatre has been the official home of the Singapore Symphony Orchestra from its formation in 1979. T Woolner's statue of Sir Stamford Raffles (1887) which originally stood on the Padang was moved to its present position in front of the Hall in 1919.

1856–1862

St Andrews Cathedral

St. Andrews Road / Coleman Street

Architect // Lt-Col R MacPherson PWD

Lieutenant-Colonel Ronald MacPherson of the Public Works Department designed the present building. It replaced an earlier church on the site, designed by J T Thomson (1842), and an even earlier one by GD Coleman (1835–1836). The style chosen was Early English of the 12th Century, and the church resembles Netley Abbey in Hampshire, which MacPherson had apparently seen as a young man. The details were kept as plain as possible, so that they were within the capabilities of the convict workforce. The Lord Bishop of Calcutta laid the foundation stone on 4th March 1856 and it was consecrated as the Anglican Cathedral in 1862. It is one of a number of important civic buildings that fringe the Padang, and was gazetted as a National Monument in June 1973.

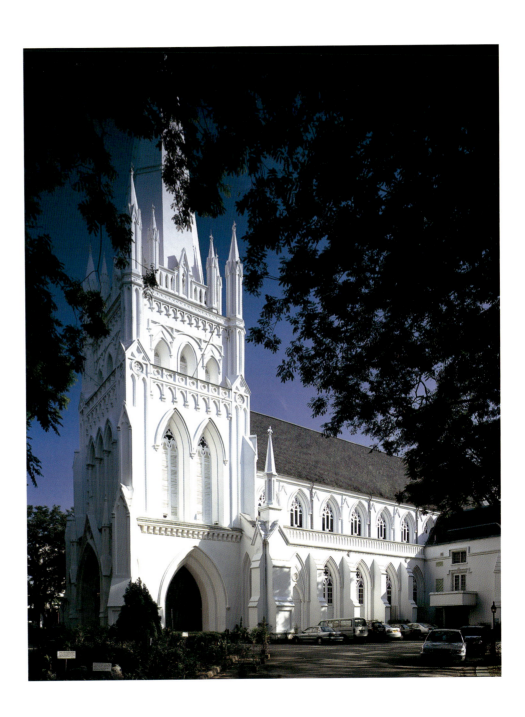

1865 – 1867

St Joseph's Institute

renamed the Singapore Art Museum in 1996

Bras Basah Road

Architect // Brother Lothaire

Additions and alterations Father R P Ch Nain 1906, by Brother Michael 1912. Conservation and adaptive reuse by PWD Consultants Ltd 1995.

St Joseph's Institute, a Roman Catholic boys school founded in 1852, originally operated from a small chapel on this site erected in 1832. The central block of the present building was completed in 1867 to the designs of the priest-architect Brother Lothaire, and the distinctive curved wings with their deep shaded arcades, designed by another priest-architect Father Nain, were added in 1906. In the mid-1990s the school moved to larger modern premises, and in 1992 the building was gazetted as a National Monument. Four years later on 20th January 1996, following major conservation work and adaptations, the former school building started a new life as the Singapore Art Museum, housing the nation's Modern Art collection.

HISTORICAL PHOTOGRAPH COURTESY OF SINGAPORE ARCHIVES

1864 – 1867

Empress Place Building

renamed Asian Civilisations Museum Empress Place in 2003

1 Empress Place

Architect // JFA McNair, Chief Engineers Office

Conservation and adaptive reuse by DP Architects Pte Ltd and Didier Repellin in 1988 – 1989 and by CPG Consultants Pte Ltd 2001 – 2003. Interiors by Forum Architects

The Empress Place Building was originally intended to be the Government Court House, but it subsequently housed the Chamber of the Straits Legislative Council and later still, the Immigration Department and the Singapore Registry of Citizenship. The masonry structure was built by Indian convict labour between 1864 and 1867. Additions were made in 1879 and 1888, and again in the early 1900s. In 1988 the elegant Georgian building was extensively renovated, and numerous insensitive post-war additions were removed. It began a new life as a museum displaying Chinese art and archaeology in April 1989. Ten years later it was again extensively renovated and reopened in March 2003 as the flagship of the Asian Civilisations Museum.

1867 – 1918 // A CROWN COLONY - THE CROSSROADS OF SOUTHEAST ASIA

On 1st April 1867 Singapore became a British Crown Colony, directly under the Colonial Office in London. This followed a prolonged campaign by a radical group of merchants in Singapore to cast off the restraining hand of the Government's India Office in Calcutta.

In 1869, the Suez Canal was opened and Singapore rapidly developed as an *entrepôt* for the whole of Asia. The steady conversion of sailing ships to steamships meant that trade was no longer subject to the vagaries of the monsoon winds, and the colony experienced boom conditions. The boom was further fuelled by the demand for rubber for motor car tyres and for tin for the canning industry. Malaya was the key supplier of both materials. Singapore became the centre of the Mecca pilgrim trade, and 7,000 Indonesians who made the pilgrimage each year left from Singapore. The population of Singapore rose from 50,000 in 1850 to 200,000 in 1900.

The power and grandeur of the British Empire in Victoria's reign was conveyed through neo-Renaissance architecture, and if GD Coleman dominated the first half of the 19th Century with his Palladian style buildings, then Major JFA McNair of the Public Works Department can be seen as the major influence on the architecture of the second half of that century.[17] As noted earlier he designed the Empress Place Building (1864) and in 1869 he was the architect of Government House (now known as the Istana).

The Colonial Office in London favoured neo-Classical architecture as a means of 'impressing the natives' and that is what McNair, and other Government officers, including Bennett, McCullum, McRitchie, and later, Tomlinson gave them. The design of public buildings followed the Victorian style in London.

The Governor of the newly created Colony was Sir Harry St. George Ord, formerly Governor of Bermuda. One of his initial acts was to commission an official residence for the representative of the British Government (1867 – 1869). Designed by Major McNair the Government House (Istana) is a large well-proportioned two-storey neo-Classical mansion sited in an elevated location off Orchard Road. It is now the official residence of the President of Singapore.

Major McNair was also involved, with Major H E McCallum, in the design of Raffles Library and Museum (1886-1887). The building, which would later be renamed the National Museum, was opened in 1887 to mark Queen Victoria's Diamond Jubilee.

MERCHANTS AND ENTREPRENEURS

The second half of the 19th Century saw the rise of several affluent Chinese business families, some of them headed by men who had relatively humble beginnings but who had worked hard and amassed fortunes. Many donated a portion of their wealth to fund temples and clan houses.

The pauper hospital of Tan Tock Seng (1844) at Pearl's Hill was funded by Tan Tock Seng JP, a prominent Hokkien merchant and philanthropist who was Straits Settlements Consul General and Special Commissioner for Siam. The money to build the Tan Si Chong Su Temple (1876) in Magazine Road was donated by Tan Kim Cheng (1829 – 1892) and Tan Beng Swee (1828 – 1884), both descendents of Tan Tock Seng. Another wealthy philanthropist, Gan Eng Seng, funded the Thong Chai Medical Hall (1892).

Some Chinese merchants displayed their wealth with impressive dwellings. Tan Yeok Nee, a wealthy gambler and pepper merchant, built a Chinese courtyard house in Clemenceau Avenue (1885) using materials and artefacts from China. Another house, built in Tai Gin Road in the 1880s by businessman Boey Chuan Poh, later became the headquarters of the Singapore branch of the Tong Meng Hui (Revolutionary Alliance) headed by Dr Sun Yat Sen.

In the early 20th Century, the transformation of Emerald Hill into a residential suburb started when the land came into the ownership of Seah Boon Kang and Seah Eng Kiat. The former nutmeg plantation was sub-divided into narrow lots, and over the next thirty years wealthy Peranakans and Teochew Straits-born Chinese built exquisite town houses, similar in their spatial organisation to the shophouse.

Arab traders, teachers and missionaries played a significant role in the Malay Archipelago. Prominent families such as the Alkaffs, the

Al-Juneids and the Alsagoffs controlled the Mecca pilgrim traffic and much of the inter-archipelago sailing trade in the 19th Century. The first member of the Alsagoff family to settle in Singapore was Syed Abdul Rahman Alsagoff, the 33rd descendent of the Prophet Mohammed[18] who arrived in 1824 from what is now the Peoples Republic of South Yemen. The Alsagoff family prospered, and in 1912 endowed the Madrasah Alsagoff in Kampong Glam. It continues to teach the Islamic religion and the Arabic language.

Other entrepreneurs were benefiting from the economic success of the colony. The Armenian merchant Aristarchus Moses arrived in 1820, the first of a small but wealthy community. Three Armenian brothers, Martin, Tigran and Arshak Sarkies opened the elegant Raffles Hotel (1886) in Beach Road. Extensions were carried out in 1899, designed by the architectural firm of Swan and Maclaren. The architectural style of the main building of Raffles Hotel is Palladian with a central section surmounted by a triangular pediment. The design was the work of R A J Bidwell, a graduate of the AA in London, who joined Swan and Mclaren in 1895.

Swan and Maclaren were also the architects of Atbara, in Gallop Road, the residence of John Burkinshaw (1898), a lawyer and one of the founders of the Straits Steamship Company. An eclectic building that owes something to the Arts and Crafts movement; it later became the French Embassy.

Bidwell drew up the plans for the Teutonia Club (1900) in Scotts Road, the social hub of the German community in Singapore. The architecture of this building was in a much more flamboyant late-Victorian language than the restrained elevations of Raffles Hotel. Later it became the Goodwood Park Hotel.

Building of government infrastructure continued at a great pace as the 19th Century drew to a close. The construction method preferred by James McRitchie, the Municipal Engineer (1883–1895) and designer of the Telok Ayer Market (1894) in Telok Ayer Street, was prefabricated cast iron, made in this instance by the Glasgow firm of P&W Maclellan.

Other public buildings adopted the neo-Classical style sanctioned by the Colonial Office. The Jinriksha Building (1903) in Neil Road was the base from which the city's riksha pullers operated.[19] Samuel Tomlinson, the Municipal Engineer, with D M Craik the Municipal Architect, designed this well-proportioned building, which has a square tower and an octagonal cupola.

A small but influential Jewish community has existed in Singapore from the early days of the settlement - a synagogue was shown on the 1846 map of the town. A larger place of worship, the Chesed-El Synagogue (1905), was funded by Manasseh Meyer and designed by Swan and Maclaren. Meyer was a wealthy man who served as a Municipal Councillor from 1893 to 1900, and was knighted for his services in 1906.

Eden Hall, a large residence built in 1904 for another Jewish businessman, Ezekial Saleh Manasseh, the proprietor of S Manasseh and Company, Gunny Rice and Opium Merchants of Calcutta, was built in an ornate Edwardian-Classical Revival style. The house was acquired after Manasseh's death in 1945 by the British Government as a residence for their High Commissioner.

By 1904 Swan and Maclaren were the largest architectural firm in Singapore. R A J Bidwell dominated the work of the firm between 1895 and 1914. In addition to the Chesed-El Synagogue they were the architects for the Singapore Cricket Club extension (1907), and for Tao Nan School (1910) in Armenian Street.

The Central Fire Station (1909) in Hill Street is attributed to D C Rae, an Assistant Architect in the Municipal Council of Singapore, though William Ferguson signed the plans. It is a combination of red brick and white render in horizontal bands, and it signalled a shift from the Palladian and neo-Classical themes.

This shift was also apparent in St. George's Church (1911) in Tanglin designed by Captain (later Lt. Col.) Stanbury, who was a Royal Engineer's officer and also a Fellow of the RIBA. Its scale and tactile qualities appear to have been influenced by the Arts and Crafts tradition in Edwardian England.

It is evident that there were differences of opinion in London on architectural styles to be adopted in the colonies. Around this time Sir Edwin Lutyens was engaged in a contentious debate on the architectural language to be adopted for Government offices in the new Indian capital of New Delhi (1911).

The period from the start of Queen Victoria's reign in 1837 to the outbreak of World War I saw the British Empire extend its influence and power. The Empire covered one fifth of the world's land area and contained one quarter of the world's population. Singapore's architecture in this period reflected the prevailing values of the British Colonial Office.

1867–1869

The Istana
formerly Government House
Orchard Road / Cavenagh Road

Architect // Major JFA McNair, Public Works Department

This large well-proportioned two-storey house, employing Ionic, Doric and Corinthian classical orders, was designed by Major JFA McNair of the Public Works Department for Governor Ord in 1869. It is sited in an elevated location with fine views of the extensive landscaped grounds and gardens, which include a nine-hole golf course. The house was the official residence of 21 British Governors prior to independence, and is now the official residence of the President of the Republic of Singapore. The grounds are open to the public on four days of the year New Year's Day, Chinese New Year, Hari Raya and Deepavali.

HISTORICAL PHOTOGRAPH COURTESY OF SINGAPORE ARCHIVES

1868–1869

Cavenagh Bridge

Singapore River

Architect // Public Works Department

This is the oldest bridge across the Singapore River, and was built to commemorate the change of status of Singapore to a Crown Colony in 1867. The steel components of the bridge were prefabricated in Glasgow by P&W MacLellan, and shipped out to be erected by Indian convict labour. Named after Major-General William Orfeur Cavenagh, the last Governor answerable to the Government in India (1859–1867), the bridge linked the Commercial Square to the government district. It was unfortunately not sufficiently high to permit fully laden *tongkangs* to pass beneath it at high tide, which created some inconvenience. Today it functions as a pedestrian link from Empress Place to the city.

1876

Tan Si Chong Su Temple

15 Magazine Road

The money to build this single-storey Hokkien temple was donated by Tan Kim Cheng (1829–1892) and Tan Beng Swee (1828–1884), both descendents of Tan Tock Seng, a prominent Hokkien merchant and philanthropist who was Straits Settlements Consul General and Special Commissioner for Siam. The ornate temple is also known as Po Chiak Kung and Tan Seng Haw, and it serves as a centre for the Tan clan. Many of the materials used in the construction of the ornate roof, carved columns and screens were imported from the Chinese mainland. It is especially rich in ceramic flowers and in gilt-covered carvings, mouldings and murals.

1877–1878

Orchard Road Presbyterian Church

Orchard Road / Penang Road

The original church was built on land granted by the Governor of Singapore in 1875. The proportions of the neo-Palladian architecture of the original were excellent. Later additions and alterations in 1921, 1925, 1935, 1954, 1975 and 1986, which extended the wings, added a church hall, and enlarged and modernised the structure, have not improved the original but they have not seriously marred its visual quality. The church is a landmark in the Bras Basah area, not so much for its size as for its scale and detail in what has become a very commercial area boasting numerous inward orientated shopping malls, hotels and office towers.

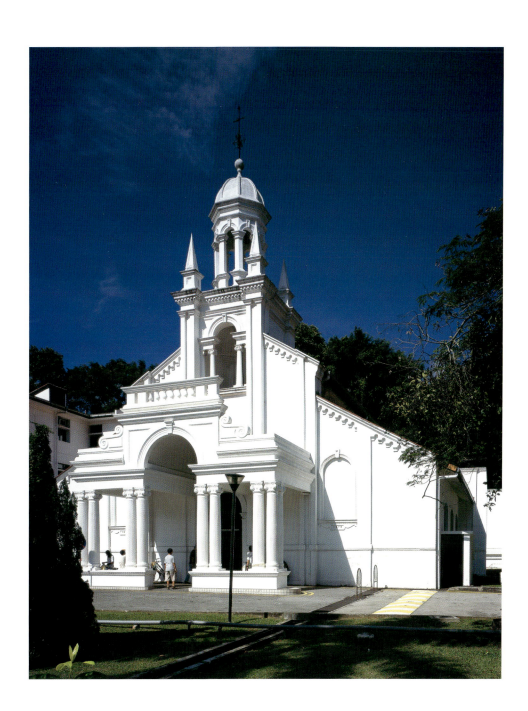

1880

Sun Yat Sen Villa

12 Tai Gin Road

Renovations by Chung and Wong 1938
Renovations by DP Architects Pte Ltd 2001

Built in the 1880s by businessman Boey Chuan Poh to house his mistress Bin Chan. In the early 1900s the house became the headquarters of the Singapore branch of the Tong Meng Hui (Revolutionary Alliance) headed by Dr Sun Yat Sen, who brought to an end 267 years of Qing rule in China following the 1911 revolution. Sun Yat Sen stayed in the house on three occasions from 1900 to 1906. The Singapore Chinese Chamber of Commerce and Industry subsequently acquired the house, and it was maintained as a memorial to the man who became the first provisional President of the Republic of China. It was closed in 1997, and following a four-year restoration project was re-opened to the public on November 12th 2001.

1884

Singapore Cricket Club

Connaught Drive

Architect // Swan and Maclaren

The Singapore Cricket Cub was founded in 1852. The pavilion has been rebuilt several times, but the 1884 building designed by Swan and Maclaren forms the core of the current clubhouse. It was completed in 1907 and wings were added in 1922. It is an anachronism in modern Singapore to see 22 individuals (mainly Caucasian and Indian) perspiring in the midday sun, and playing cricket on one of the most valuable pieces of real estate in the world, situated on the edge of the Central Business District. The pavilion has a broad verandah, with wrought iron balustrades, overlooking the Padang (field) where sportsmen and women congregate in the early evening as they have for more than 150 years.

1885

Tan Yeok Nee House
renamed as The University of Chicago Graduate Business School in 2001

207 Clemenceau Avenue / Penang Road

Alterations and additions RSP Architects Planners and Engineers 2001

Tan Yeok Nee, a wealthy gambler and pepper merchant, built this house using granite columns and timber carvings from China. It later became the Station Master's house when the railway line was constructed along Clemenceau Avenue. Subsequently it was the residence of the Bishop of Singapore, a boarding school for girls and the headquarters of the Salvation Army. In World War II the Japanese Army requisitioned the building. It is the only remaining example of a Chinese courtyard house in Singapore, and in 2000–2001 it was restored and adapted for use as The University of Chicago Graduate School of Business.

1886

Raffles Hotel

1 Beach Road / 328 North Bridge Road

Alterations and additions by Swan and Maclaren in 1899 and by Architects 61 in 1989-1991.

Three Armenian brothers, Martin, Tigran and Arshak Sarkies, who hailed from Julfa (in what is now known as Turkey), opened Raffles Hotel. They initially purchased a house on the present site in 1886, and Swan and Maclaren designed extensions in 1899. The architectural style of the main building is Palladian with a central section surmounted by a triangular pediment.

In 1989 Raffles Hotel (1886) Pte Ltd (a subsidiary of DBS Land) committed S$160 million to restoring the building to the style and ambience of the 1920s, when the hotel was in its heyday. The restoration of the main building and extensions in the style of the original were carried out under the direction of Architects 61 Pte Ltd.

1886–1887

National Museum
Stamford Road

Architect // HE McCallum and JFA McNair
Public Works Department

Alterations and additions Public Works
Department 1906, 1916, 1926.

The museum was opened in 1887 to mark Queen Victoria's Diamond Jubilee. It was originally known as the Raffles Library and Museum, and was established as a museum of natural history and anthropology. Subsequent alterations and additions were carried out in 1906, 1916 and 1926. A library wing and a south wing were added. The Classical style building has a prominent dome, and is a landmark in the Bras Basah area. In 1960 it became a museum of history, ethnology and art and was renamed The National Museum. Further alterations and additions commenced in 2002, directed by CPG Consultants Pte Ltd.

1892

Thong Chai Medical Hall

50 Eu Tong Sen Street/Wayang Street

Renovations by Pan-Malaysian Group Architects and Lee Sian Teck 1974–1979. Conservation and adaptive reuse by Design Environment Group 2001–2002

The Thong Chai Medical Institution was set up in 1867 and moved to the present building in 1892. A wealthy philanthropist Gan Eng Seng funded the Medical Hall, and its purpose was to distribute free medical care. It was built in the form of a traditional Chinese urban dwelling with two internal courtyards. The building was acquired by the Government in 1972 and was gazetted as a National Monument on June 28th 1973. It underwent extensive renovation and for some years was used as an antiques shop. In 2002 it was restored and reopened as - Le Bar - an up-market dining experience. It was short-lived, closing just one year later.

1894

Telok Ayer Market
renamed as Lau Pa Sat in 1996
235 Telok Ayer Street/Raffles Quay

Architect // James McRitchie

Conservation and adaptive reuse by William Lim Associates and Architectural Restoration Consultants Ltd in 1992 and Quek Associates in 1996.

The reclamation of Telok Ayer Bay was carried out in 1879. Telok Ayer Market was erected on the reclaimed land near the new shoreline. It is a cast iron structure octagonal in plan, and was prefabricated by P&W Maclellan in Glasgow and erected by Riley Hargreaves and Co. (now United Engineers Ltd). The original use of the market was to sell fresh fish, fruit and vegetables. The market was closed from 1985 to 1986 as it was affected by underground work on the MRT. It was dismantled and subsequently rebuilt on the same site as a Festival Market, reopening in 1992. It has since undergone another makeover and is now a popular food centre known as Lau Pa Sat.

1898

Atbara
5 Gallop Road

Architect // Swan and Maclaren

Designed by RAJ Bidwell of Swan and Maclaren as the residence of John Burkinshaw, a lawyer and one of the founders of the Straits Steamship Company, Atbara later became the French Embassy. It fulfilled this role until 1999, when the embassy was relocated to a modern purpose-built structure at the junction of Cluny Road and Bukit Timah Road. Atbara is an eclectic building, incorporating a Moorish-style arcaded 1st storey, a porte-cochère that appears to be derived from the Arts and Crafts movement and a rambling arrangement of rooms. It is located at the top of a gentle grassed slope at the rear of the Botanic Gardens and seems to exist in a time warp. It is in a severe state of decay and in need of restoration work if it is to be saved for posterity.

1900

Goodwood Park Hotel
22 Scotts Road

Architect // RAJ Bidwell of Swan and Maclaren

alterations and additions by Cheng Heng Tat Associates 1976

RAJ Bidwell drew up the plans for the original building just one year after he designed the Raffles Hotel. It couldn't be more different, its architecture is in a much more flamboyant style than the restrained elevations of the Raffles Hotel. It was originally the Teutonia Club, a meeting place for the German community in Singapore. The Australian Army occupied it immediately after World War II for the purpose of investigating Japanese war crimes. It later became the Goodwood Park Hotel and the flagship property of the Goodwood Hotel Group.

1901

Emerald Hill Road

The transformation of Emerald Hill into a stylish residential suburb started in 1901 when the land came into the ownership of Seah Boon Kang and Seah Eng Kiat. The former nutmeg plantation was subdivided into lots, and over the next thirty years it was progressively built up along the slope of Emerald Hill Road, mainly by wealthy Teochew Straits-born Chinese and Peranakans. From 1965 onwards the area came under relentless pressure from the commercial and retail activities of nearby Orchard Road. The conservation of the distinctive row houses was inspired by the writings of Lee Kip Lin, and in 1981 the Urban Redevelopment Authority announced plans to make it a conservation area. It was gazetted on 7th July 1989.

1903

Jinriksha Building

Neil Road

Architect // Samuel Tomlinson
with DM Craik

The first rickshas arrived from Shanghai in 1880, and by 1919 20,000 ricksha pullers were pulling 9,000 rikshas in the city centre. The Jinriksha Building was the administrative base from which they operated. Samuel Tomlinson, the Municipal Engineer, with DM Craik the Municipal Architect, designed the building. It is well-proportioned with a square tower and an octagonal cupola above a curved pediment and Ionic pilasters, and successfully terminates South Bridge Road. The building has undergone several rounds of conservation, and the original exposed brick façades of the building have been revealed. It is currently used as a seafood restaurant and, curiously, the headquarters of the Tampines Rovers Football Club.

1904

Eden Hall – British High Commissioner's Residence

28 Nassim Road

This house was originally built for a Jewish businessman Ezekial Saleh Manasseh, the proprietor of S Manasseh and Company, Gunny Rice and Opium Merchants of Calcutta. For several years it was leased to a Mrs Campbell who ran a boarding house. Manasseh lived in the house from 1918 until his death in 1945. It was later acquired by the British Government as a residence for their High Commissioner and underwent major restoration work in 1993. The style of the house is ornate late Edwardian-Classical Revival. There is elaborately decorated plaster relief work on the parapet and walls. Eden Hall is situated within a splendid garden with a number of mature trees.

1905

Chesed-El Synagogue

Oxley Rise

Architect // RAJ Bidwell of Swan and Maclaren

There has been a Jewish community in Singapore since 1830. A synagogue was shown on the 1846 map of the town, by which time there were 6 Jewish merchant houses. By 1910 the number had grown to 500. The Chesed-El Synagogue was privately funded by Manasseh Meyer, and was built close to Belle Vue, his residence in Killiney Road, a beautiful house demolished in 1982. Meyer was a wealthy man who served as a Municipal Councillor from 1893 to 1900, and was knighted for his services in 1906. The building is a well-proportioned Classical composition by RAJ Bidwell of Swan and Maclaren, which sits comfortably on the hillside. It is one of two synagogues in Singapore, the other being Maghain Aboth in Waterloo Street, built in 1878.

1909

Central Fire Station

62 Hill Street

Architect // DC Rae, Municipal Council of Singapore

Restoration and additions by CPG Consultants 2001

The Central Fire Station was completed in 1909, almost two decades after a Fire Brigade was established in Singapore. The building is a combination of rustic red brick and white render in horizontal bands, sometimes referred to as the 'blood and bandage' style popular in Edwardian England. It indicated a shift from the familiar Classical architecture of government buildings in Singapore and is attributed to DC Rae, an Assistant Architect in the Municipal Council of Singapore, although William Ferguson signed the plans. The handsome building is still in use almost a century later, and CPG Consultants carried out restoration and sensitive Modern additions in 2001.

1910

Tao Nan School

renamed as Asian Civilisations Museum
Armenian Street in 2003

39 Armenian Street

Architect // Swan and Maclaren

Alterations and additions by PWD Consultants
Pte Ltd 1996

Tao Nan School was founded in 1906, and three local Chinese benefactors financed this small but elegant symmetrical building with arched verandahs, fluted pilasters and green glazed balusters. It also boasted a magnificent light-filled central atrium and a grand staircase. It was the first school in Singapore to introduce Mandarin as the medium of instruction. The school moved to new premises in 1984, and the premises stood empty for more than a decade. The building was acquired by the Government, and after major conservation work by PWD Consultants, opened as The Asian Civilisations Museum in 1997. It has ten galleries on three levels and now focuses on the display of Peranakan culture.

1911

St George's Church, Tanglin

Minden Road

Architect // Captain William Henry Stanbury
extension by Design International 1981

The garrison church of St George's at Tanglin served the British Army and their families from 1911 until 1971. It was designed by Captain (later Lt. Col.) Stanbury, a Royal Engineer's officer and a Fellow of the RIBA. The worship hall seats 650, and relies on natural ventilation aided by suspended ceiling fans. It has semi-circular arched brick openings with a well-proportioned nave, and a roof with exposed timber trusses that may have been influenced by the work of Edwin Lutyens. After World War II the church was rededicated on Sunday November 10th 1946 when Field Marshall Montgomery read the lesson. When the British Forces withdrew, the church was handed over to the Anglican diocese.

1912

Madrasah Alsagoff

111 Jalan Sultan

additions and alterations by Architect
Yong Kok Choo

The first member of the Alsagoff family to settle in Singapore was Syed Abdul Rahman Alsagoff, who arrived in 1824 from what is now the Peoples Republic of South Yemen. He set up the trading company of Alsagoff and Company. At the beginning of the 20th Century three Arab families - Alsagoff, Al-junied and Alkaff - controlled the Mecca pilgrim traffic and much of the inter-archipelago sailing ship trade. The Alsagoff family endowed Alsagoff Arab School and it was originally a three storey building accessed by a central staircase. The pediment, which has the appearance of a Dutch gable, is inscribed with Arabic script and the date 1912.

1918 – 1942 // THE TWILIGHT OF THE BRITISH EMPIRE

The early 1920s saw a growth in the number of spacious houses built for colonial administrators. These houses in areas such as Adam Park and Goodwood Hill, designed by anonymous (military) engineers, combined the familiar language of the English Tudor cottage with the climatic responsiveness of the Malay *kampong* house on stilts. They were popularly referred to as Black-and-White Houses. Set in spacious gardens, they established increased spatial separation of the colonial civil servants and the indigenous culture. Europeans tended to distance themselves from the 'locals', to frequent their own social clubs and to surround themselves with domestic servants.

The typical Singapore shophouse continued to be built. Near the junction of Koon Seng Road with Joo Chiat Road are two rows of terrace houses built in 1929. They are highly ornate with splendid plasterwork, and illustrate some of the best eclectic Straits Chinese architecture of the inter-war years.

Swan and Maclaren continued to dominate the architectural profession in the post-World War 1 period, and captured many of the important commissions. The Sultan Mosque (1924–1928) designed by Denis Santry of Swan and Maclaren, is a significant landmark in Kampong Glam. New Zealander Frank Gordon Lundon joined the practice in 1918. He was conversant with cast iron, structural steel and reinforced concrete construction, and was responsible for projects such as the Hongkong and Shanghai Bank (1922) and the Singapore Turf Club (1934).

Another practice that flourished for a short period from the mid-1920s until the early 1930s was Keys and Dowdeswell. They were a Shanghai based firm of architects who came to Singapore when they won a competition for the Fullerton Building, completed in 1928. The Classical style building served for many years as the General Post Office. In 1997 it was acquired by Sino Land Company and adapted for a new use as the Fullerton Hotel. Keys and Dowdeswell were also responsible for the College of Medicine Building (1923–1926) at Singapore General Hospital in Outram/New Bridge Road. It has an imposing Classical façade of Doric columns.

Another public building, the neo-Classical style Municipal Building (1926–1929) in St. Andrews Road, later renamed City Hall, was designed by A Gordon and FD Meadows, respectively the Architect and Assistant Architect of the Municipal Council of Singapore.

Classicism lingered on for a few more years and Frank Dorrington Ward of the Public Works Department turned out two neo-Classical buildings that were the last dramatic flourish of an empire in decline. The Hill Street Building (1934–1936), also known as the Hill Street Police Station, has a slightly forbidding façade with corbelled loggias and balconies, while the main façade of the Supreme Court (1937–1939), which was the last public building in Singapore to be designed in the Classical style, has a very heavy appearance. It has been referred to as the "last example of British imperial architecture in Singapore."[20]

MODERN ARCHITECTURE IN SINGAPORE

Modern architecture arrived in Singapore soon after WWI. Much of the early 20th Century Modern architecture was concerned with creating affordable dwellings for workers. Accompanying moral and social criticism by Ruskin and Morris were the utopian ideas of Ebenezer Howard (1898) and Tony Garnier (1901–1904), the Siedlungen housing of Ernst May (1926–1929) and JP Oud's Kiethoek housing of 1925.

The Singapore Improvement Trust (SIT) was formed in 1927 and operated until 1959. The SIT initially had limited powers to tackle housing problems but in 1932 its remit was extended to carry out low-rental housing schemes. The young architects of the SIT were very much aware of developments in Europe. The Tiong Bahru Estate (1936–1954) was designed by James Milner Frazer, who had previously worked with the London County Council Architectural Department. It was Singapore's first public housing estate and was directly related to the values implicit in the European models.

Frank Brewer arrived in Singapore in 1919 with a degree in architecture from Kings College, London. He worked with Swan and Maclaren before setting up his own practice in 1932. The design of 31 and 33 Club Street (1932) is attributed to Brewer, whose name became synonymous with architecture in transition from the Classical style to Modernism. Another house by Brewer at 23 Ridout Road (1934) is one of several he designed that creates a connection between the Arts and Crafts movement and Modernism. Later he designed the first 'skyscraper' in Singapore, the Cathay Building (1939).

Swan and Maclaren were responsible for the design of the Singapore Railway Station (1932–1937) in Keppel Road. It is the work of DS Petrovitch, a Serbian who trained at the AA in London and who joined Swan and Maclaren in 1929. Eliel Saarinen's Helsinki Station (1910–1914) is thought to have influenced the reinforced concrete building. The firm also designed the Great Southern Hotel (1927), an early Modern landmark in Chinatown.

Frank Dorrington Ward of the PWD showed that he too was able to turn his hand to a Modernist design. Clifford Pier (1933) has an impressive interior with elegant concrete arches providing a column free space befitting a transportation terminal. Kallang Airport (1937), also attributed to Ward, was the first civil airport in Singapore. It too was in a Modernist language and has an affinity with the work of Erich Mendelsohn (1887–1953) in Europe.

If public architecture was embracing the Modern Movement, private architects were also beginning to experiment. Chung and Wong, a local firm formed in 1920 were responsible for the house of Aw Boon Par in Nassim Road (1930) and the Happy World Stadium (1937). Ho Kwong Yew (1903–1902) was one of the leading proponents of the Modern Movement in the 1930s. From 1926 to 1930 he worked with Chung and Wong before setting up his own practice. The Chee Guan Chiang House (1938) in Grange Road, designed by Ho, is distinctly Modern in its language and was possibly influenced by the architecture of the Weissenhof Siedlung (1927) in Stuttgart and by FRS Yorke's influential book 'The Modern House', published in 1934.

The years between World War I and World War II witnessed the gradual implosion of the British Empire, culminating in the surrender of the Singapore garrison to the invading Japanese army in 1942. This event alone was to have a profound effect on the relationship between the colonisers and the colonised. The myth of European invincibility was shattered, and the entrenched belief of the white races in their superiority was undermined. Added to this was a growing belief among some of the British that having an empire was morally unjustified. The way was paved for the rise of nationalism and the birth of the *Merdeka* (freedom) movement in the post-war period. A 'wind of change' blew through the colonies in India, Africa and Asia.

The Supreme Court 1937–1939

1920s
Goodwood Hill

The early 1920s saw a growth in the number of spacious houses built for colonial administrators. These houses, designed by anonymous (military) engineers, combined the familiar language of the English Tudor cottage with the climatic responsiveness of the Malay *kampong* house on stilts. They are popularly referred to as Black-and-White Houses. Set in spacious gardens, they established the spatial separation of the colonial civil servants and the indigenous culture. Today these houses are frequently the homes of a new elite consisting of CEO's and managers of multi-national companies. Social divisions are still apparent, though they are now tied into the global economy rather than the dominance of a colonial elite.

1923–1926

The College of Medicine Building (Ministry of Health)

Outram/New Bridge Road

Architect // Keys and Dowdeswell

The foundation stone of the College of Medicine Building was laid in September 1923, and the Governor Sir Laurence N Guillermaud officially opened the building in February 1926. It is a reinforced concrete building with an imposing façade of Doric columns in the ponderous Classicism favoured by Major PH Keys. One jarring detail is the appearance of a row of dormer lights above the entablature. The bas-relief work around the main entrance and on the walls on either side illustrates scenes of the teaching and practice of medicine. Over the central doorway is a bas-relief of an eagle and a wreath. In 1984 the College of Medicine was extensively restored and adapted to house the Academy of Medicine and the Council of General Practitioners.

1927

Great Southern Hotel

renamed as Yue Hwa Chinese Products in 1996

70 Eu Tong Sen Street

Architect // Swan and Maclaren

Conservation and adaptive reuse by Meng Ta Cheang of OD Architects 1996.

A landmark in Chinatown, The Great Southern Hotel, was said to be as popular a destination for Chinese visitors as the Raffles Hotel was for Europeans. The architectural language was that of the Modern Movement, strictly functional with steel frame windows and planar surfaces. Indeed the grey coloured building appeared somewhat austere. The loggia on the uppermost floor was a little lighter with the use of cast iron balustrades and brackets and there was extensive use of green glass. There was a popular Chinese restaurant on the fourth floor, and a teahouse was located on the roof terrace. The hotel was conserved and adapted by OD Architects in 1996. A new extension was added to the rear linked by a four-storey atrium.

1924 – 1928

Sultan Mosque
North Bridge Road

Architect // Swan and Maclaren

The Sultan Mosque, located at the end of Bussorah Street in Kampong Glam, is a significant landmark in the area. It was built from 1924–1928 to designs by Dennis Santry of Swan and Maclaren on the site of an earlier mosque on the site, built around 1824. The land was originally part of Sultan Hussein Shah's 23-hectare enclave. The Sultan Mosque is the focus of the Muslim faith in Singapore and is a mixture of Classical, Moorish, Turkish and Persian themes, which together form a recognisable Islamic style. There are some excellent urban spaces clustered around the mosque, and the building forms the focus of the vista along Bussorah Street.

1919 – 1928

The Fullerton Building (General Post Office)
renamed The Fullerton Hotel in 1999

Fullerton Square

Architect // Keys and Dowdeswell

Conservation and adaptive reuse by PWD and David Tay and Associates in 1985 and by Architects 61 Pte Ltd in 1997 – 2000.

The Fullerton Building takes its name from Robert Fullerton, the Governor of Singapore from 1826 to 1829, and sits on the site of Fort Fullerton, built in 1829 to defend the entrance to the Singapore River. The fort was demolished in 1873. Keys and Dowdeswell were a Shanghai based firm of architects who came to Singapore when they won a competition for the Fullerton Building in 1919. The building is in a Classical style with fluted Doric columns on a heavy base, and served with dignity as the Central Post Office. In 1997 it was acquired by Sino Land Company and was conserved and adapted for a new use as The Fullerton Hotel.

1926–1929

City Hall
formerly the Municipal Building
St Andrews Road

Architect // A Gordon and FD Meadows:
Municipal Council of Singapore

The neo-Classical style City Hall was designed by A Gordon and FD Meadows, respectively the Architect and Assistant Architect of the Municipal Council of Singapore. The building has a substantial rusticated basement with a wide flight of steps leading to the first storey entrance. It is an asymmetrical building with a row of tall Doric columns, which form a colonnade supporting a horizontal entablature. The windows are set well back between the columns. The steps of the City Hall have witnessed many historic events. In June 1959 the Peoples Action Party (PAP) held a *Merkeka* (Freedom) rally in front of City Hall immediately after the elections when Lee Kuan Yew's party won 49 out of the 51 parliamentary seats to form an unassailable majority in a self-governing Singapore.

1929
Koon Seng Road

Koon Seng Road is named after Cheong Koon Seng, an auctioneer and estate agent who received training with Powell and Co., before setting up his own firm. With his brother, Cheong Koon Hong, he was also proprietor of the Star Opera Company and they built the Theatre Royal in North Bridge Road. Near the junction with Joo Chiat Road, Koon Seng Road has two rows of terrace houses. They are highly ornate with Malay fretwork at the eaves, decorated entablatures above the second floor windows, bas-relief work below the windows, Ionic pilasters to the decorative corbels, and carved *pintu pagars*. Koon Seng Road illustrates some of the best eclectic Straits Chinese architecture of the inter-war years.

1929–1930

Capital Building

Stamford Road / North Bridge Road

Architect // Keys and Dowdeswell

The Capital Building was originally built for the Namazie family, businessmen and lawyers of Persian origin who acquired the land in 1927. The building is in the rather ponderous Classical style that characterized the work of Keys and Dowdeswell. However, it turns the corner well at the junction of Stamford Road and North Bridge Road. The awkward internal planning which left pockets of unusable space spoilt the flamboyance of the corner landmark. The Capital Theatre, which lay within this maze, was given a wonderful art deco interior and a domed ceiling incorporating a tableau featuring white winged horses. Shortly after the completion of the project, the architects left Singapore in disgrace when found guilty of professional misconduct.

1932

31 and 33 Club Street

Club Street

Architect // Frank W Brewer

The design of these two distinctive houses is attributed to Frank W Brewer, whose name is synonymous in Singapore with an architecture in transition from the Classical style to Modernism. The houses are a curious combination of white planar walls and Chinese roofs and canopies. In the early 1990s Regional Development Consortium, an architectural practice, occupied No.33. In 1991 plans were drawn up to incorporate both houses into a boutique hotel to be built on the adjacent site of the former Yeung Chin School. Eventually the hotel plans were discarded and the houses became the entrance to Emerald Gardens Condominium, a large inner-city residential development on the former school site. Conservation of the building was carried out in 1992.

1931–1933

Clifford Pier

70 Collyer Quay

Architect // Frank Dorrington Ward
Public Works Department

Clifford Pier was the landing point for many of Singapore's early migrants. It was popularly known as the Red Lamp Pier. It has an impressive interior with elegant wide span reinforced-concrete arches providing a column free internal space. Smaller arched openings run along both long sides of the rectangular building, and the end gable of the pier, facing the sea, has three arched openings. The result is a splendid cool and breezy interior that gives shade and protection from the sun and rain as befits a major transportation terminal. The art deco façade of the building, facing Collyer Quay, is now detached from the life of the city by a busy highway.

1934

Ridout Road House
23 Ridout Road

Architect // Frank Brewer

Frank Brewer arrived in Singapore in 1919 with a degree in architecture from Kings College, London, and started his own practice in 1933. Brewer's houses were influenced by the architecture of Sir Edwin Lutyens, and he created a connection between the Arts and Crafts movement and Modernism. The Ridout Road House is one of a number of houses he designed in Singapore, characterised by stout brick buttresses, brick arches and rough textured render walls painted white. The architecture has some resemblance to the work of the Amsterdam School of Architecture, particularly the houses designed by De Klerk. Brewer was also responsible for the design of the Cathay Building (1939), which signalled the arrival of Modern high-rise architecture in Singapore.

1934–1936

Hill Street Building
renamed as the MITA Building in 2000

River Valley Road/Hill Street

Architect // Frank Dorrington Ward
Public Works Department

Alterations and additions by PWD Consultants
Pte Ltd 1983 and 2000

Originally designed as the Hill Street Police Station and Quarters, this corner building has a slightly forbidding neo-Classical façade with corbelled loggias and balconies. The police vacated the seven-storey property in 1980 and following renovations it became best known as the Archives and Oral History Department. It also housed the Official Consignee, the Official Trustees and the Public Receivers Office. In 2000 it again underwent substantial restoration and adaptation, and became the Ministry of Information, Communication and the Arts (MITA). The original internal courtyards have been retained and these work well in the tropical climate. Curiously the window frames, louvres and shutters have been painted in a garish spectrum of colours.

74 // 1918–1942 THE TWILIGHT OF THE BRITISH EMPIRE

1937

Kallang Airport
renamed as the Peoples Association Headquarters in 1960

Stadium Link Road

Architect // Frank Dorrington Ward
Public Works Department

alterations and additions by Architects 61 Pte Ltd in 1993

Kallang Airport was the first civil airport in Singapore. The original airport was circular, with the principal runway orientated east-west along the line of what is now Stadium Road. The Modernist language of the building, with parallel concrete floors, roof slabs and a cylindrical glass tower, can be interpreted as a metaphor for a biplane with an elevated cockpit. Many early Modernist buildings had similar imagery, with references to machines and ocean liners. The building is approached along a tree lined boulevard flanked by the old Qantas hanger and by buildings which were formerly occupied by airline offices. Since 1960 the complex has served as the headquarters of the Peoples Association (PA) who are principally concerned with youth and community development. The building was substantially renovated in 1993.

1932–1937

Singapore Railway Station

Keppel Road

Architect // Swan and Maclaren

The design of the Singapore Railway Station is attributed to DS Petrovitch, who joined the firm of Swan and Maclaren in 1929. Petrovitch was of Serbian origin and trained at the AA School of Architecture in London. Eliel Saarinen's Helsinki Station (1910–1914) in all probability influenced the reinforced concrete building. The upper walls of the lofty central waiting hall are decorated with ceramic tiles depicting colourful scenes of Malay life. The arcaded façade of the station is enlivened by four life size figures depicting Commerce, Agriculture, Industry and Shipping. The station is the southern terminus of the railway from the Malaysian capital of Kuala Lumpur. Until the early 1990s when the north-south highway linking Singapore and Kuala Lumpur was opened, the railway was the main link with Malaysia.

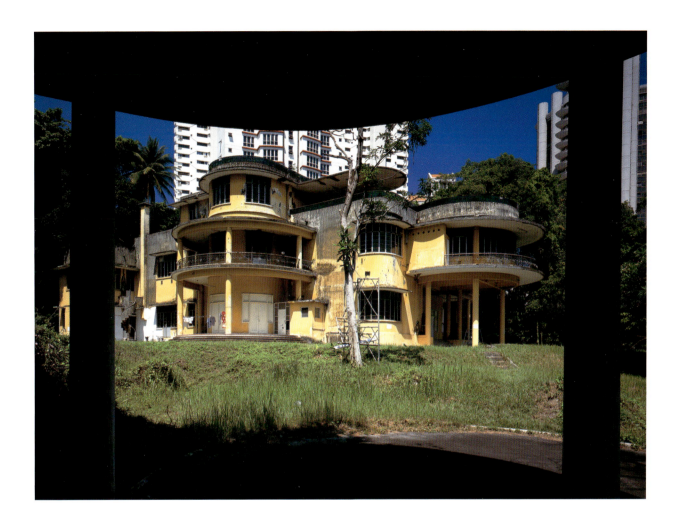

1938

Chee Guan Chiang House

Grange Road

Architect // Ho Kwong Yew

Ho Kwong Yew (1903–1942) was one of the leading lights in the Modern Movement in Singapore in the 1930s. He was a draughtsman under SD Meadows and A Gordon in the Municipal Engineers office before setting up his own practice in 1933. The Chee Guan Chiang House is distinctly Modern in its language, and is influenced by the architecture of the Weissenhof Siedlung in Stuttgart in 1927 and by Erich Mendelsohn's designs for the De La Warr Pavilion in Bexhill (UK) in 1935. The house has a plan that employs a semi-circular 'bow window' on axis in a similar manner to the Bexhill pavilion. Ho Kwong Yew was interned by the Japanese during World War II and sadly did not survive. The house has been derelict for more than a decade.

1937–1939

The Supreme Court
St. Andrews Road

Architect // Frank Dorrington Ward
Public Works Department

The Supreme Court was the last public building in Singapore to be designed in the Classical style. It replaced the Grand Hotel de l'Europe, which previously occupied the corner site overlooking the Singapore Cricket Club and the Padang. The Supreme Court building has a steel frame faced in stone, and consists of four blocks surrounding a central courtyard which houses the Law Library. The main façade has a very heavy appearance with a triangular pediment supported on Corinthian columns. The Italian stonemason Cavalieri Rodolfo Noli carried out the carving on the pediment. The Supreme Court has been referred to as the last example of British Imperial architecture in Singapore.

1942

WWII Pillbox

Pasir Panjang Road

Scattered around Singapore are remnants of World War II defences. In Pasir Panjang Road, at the entrance to the Science Park, is a solitary reinforced concrete pillbox, a memory of the bitter battles that were fought in the days before the British, under Lt General Percival, surrendered to Lt General Yamashita of the Japanese army on 15th February 1942. The 56th Regiment of the Japanese 18th Division moved up to Pasir Panjang Ridge on the 13th February 1942. The Ridge was held by the 2nd Loyals, the 1st Malay Regiment and an irregular force of Chinese. The battle lasted for 48 hours and C Company of the 1st Malay Regiment fought to the last man. The Japanese advanced through Pasir Panjang on the 14th February, and the British commander surrendered the following day.

1942–1991 // THE BIRTH OF A NATION: AN INDEPENDENT ARCHITECTURE

The British returned to Malaya after the surrender of Japanese forces but the world was changing rapidly. Within five years India had achieved independence. Lee Kuan Yew, David Marshall and other leaders were increasingly vociferous in demanding independence for Singapore.

British architectural firms re-established their offices on the cessation of hostilities. Palmer and Turner, under POG Wakeman, was one of the most prominent commercial practices. Initially set up in Shanghai, the practice came to Singapore via Hong Kong. Their Bank of China Building (1953–1954) was amongst the first high-rise tower blocks constructed in the region after World War II. Booty and Edwards and Partners resumed practice and James Ferrie left Palmer and Turner in 1953 to set up his own practice. Australian Gordon Dowsett left Palmer and Turner in the same year to join SH van Sitteran in Van Sitteran and Partners. Dowsett is credited with one of the seminal Modern buildings in Singapore, the MacPherson Road Market (1953).[21]

The Public Works Department were active in the post-war reconstruction process. Three blocks of four-storey apartments in Nassim Hill (1950–1951) were built for senior Civil Servants, the architect was KA Brundle, Chief Architect of the PWD. The Singapore Improvement Trust (SIT) also resumed work, building flats at Sago Street (1948), designed by AG Church, Prinsep Street (1948) by Lincoln Page, and Towner Road (1952) by Rolf Koren.

The post-war period saw a significant number of young Singaporean architects returning after their education in Britain, Australia and the USA. This was the advent of the local profession. Their heros and influences included Le Corbusier, Gropius, Neutra, Mies van der Rohe, Oscar Niemeyer, Louis Kahn, Maekawa, Kurokawa and others such as Roy Grounds in Australia and Peter and Alison Smithson in UK.

Ng Keng Siang was trained at the Bartlett School of Architecture in London. He was the first Singaporean to become a member of the Royal Institute of British Architects (RIBA), and his Asia Insurance Building (1954) was the tallest building in Singapore. It can be seen as the first attempt to produce Regional Modern architecture.

Alfred Wong received his architectural education at Melbourne University and founded the Alfred Wong Partnership in 1957. He was responsible for the design of the iconic National Theatre (1960–1963), which unfortunately developed structural problems and was demolished in 1986. Wong would later become the first recipient of the Singapore Institute of Architects (SIA) Gold Medal, in 1999. Wong's excellent Hotel Malaysia (1968), later renamed the Marco Polo, suffered the same fate, being demolished in 2000 to make way for serviced apartments.

In 1959 Singapore achieved self-government. A number of United Nations reports in the early 1960s formed the basis of government planning. In 1963 a UN team comprising OH Koenisberger from the UK, Charles Abrams from the USA and S Kobe of Japan submitted detailed transportation studies. Another UN mission in 1967 resulted in the establishment of the Singapore State and City Planning Unit. Slum clearance and urban renewal were given the highest priority,[22] and the Government initiated tough legislation to acquire land and properties for public purposes. The aim was to create a favourable investment climate and to build up the island's potential as an *entrepôt*. The emphasis was placed on a pragmatic approach to the renewal of the urban core, and the demolition of large numbers of buildings of architectural and historical interest was considered an acceptable and fair price to pay for 'progress'.

Many young architects returning from their studies abroad were idealistic, wishing to create architecture that celebrated the spirit of the time as the island emerged from almost a century and a half of colonial rule. In 1960, Lim Chong Keat who had carried out graduate studies under Gyorgy Kepes at MIT, and William Lim and Chen Voon Fee, both graduates of the AA School of Architecture in London, formed the practice of Malayan Architects Co-Partnership.

The Asia Insurance Building (1954)

In 1961 the firm won the competition for the National Trades Union Congress (NTUC) Conference Hall. The Modernist design, completed in 1965, was one of the most inspired buildings to emerge from that period and it was symbolic of the nationalist and socialist ideas of the time. It was the venue for the Commonwealth Heads of Government Conference in 1971, and William Lim saw it as being a combination of Paul Rudolph's service towers with Le Corbusier's Chandigarh 'umbrella' roof.[23] The building was retrofitted in 2000, and unfortunately its straightforward functional expressionism was erased in order to create air-conditioned spaces. As a piece of Modern architecture it was emasculated.

1965: SINGAPORE GAINS INDEPENDENCE. A TIME OF EXPERIMENTATION

Singapore became an independent nation in 1965. Lee Kuan Yew was the first elected Prime Minister of the city-state, and imposed a unique style of paternalistic socialism. The Government's Home Ownership Scheme was introduced, and the Housing and Development Board (HDB) set about a massive housing programme which transformed the country with the establishment of new towns. Today almost 90 percent of the Singapore population lives in high-rise public housing designed by the HDB.

Once out of the city centre this is the dominant image in the landscape. Liu Thai Ker, initially as the Chief Architect/Planner, and then CEO of the HDB (1969–1989), and finally as the CEO of the Urban Renewal Authority and Chief Planner of Singapore (1989–1992), is the individual credited with overseeing the completion of over 500,000 dwelling units and implementing the transformation of the Singapore landscape.

These were fascinating times for radicals and intellectuals intent on debating the post-colonial condition, but there were darker aspects. William Lim recalls that, "The Peoples Action Party were very single-minded in the pursuit of their political and economic objectives and if you did not agree with them you were expected to keep quiet. If you were not with them you were judged to be against them." In February 1963 in a raid named 'Operation Cold Store', the Internal Security Department detained more than 100 radicals.[24] Some of the detainees remained in prison for six years.

The first cohort of architectural students from the Singapore Polytechnic School of Architecture graduated in 1964. They too were inspired by the idealism and, in some cases, the radical mood of the time.

1964 saw the emergence of the Singapore Planning and Urban Research Group (SPUR), a multi-disciplinary society of professionals, academics and businessmen concerned with and about the urban environment. The members of SPUR had an occasionally stormy relationship with the government. The radical views expressed by the group were not always well received by the PAP Government and civil servants, and the group was quietly 'dissolved' in 1973–1974.

In the private sector experimental architecture was emerging. The ideas of the Metabolist Group which flourished in Japan in the 1960s, of the Archigram Group in UK, and the Linear City concepts of Le Corbusier and Soria y Mata in Europe were all influential and found their way into the architectural language employed by the young architects in Singapore. The Modern architecture of post-war Japan also stirred their imagination. A competition winning entry for Jurong Town Hall (1970) from Architects Team 3, provided a symbol of Singapore's industrialisation, which was centred on Jurong. It appeared to borrow ideas from Maekawa's Tokyo Festival Hall (1960).

Another practice, Design Partnership, an offshoot of Malaysian Architects Co-partnership, was successful in its proposal for the Peoples Park Complex (1970) in Eu Tong Sen Street. The big 'city room' concept owed much to the ideas of the Metabolist Group in Japan. Design Partnership followed this up with the Woh Hup Complex (1974), later renamed the Golden Mile Complex, in Beach Road. These buildings were also influenced by the Brutalist style of Peter and Alison Smithson, the interlocking geometries in the work of Alfred Neumann and by Fumihiko Maki's work on Collective Form.[25,26] Another forward-looking project was the Futura Apartments (1973–1976) by Timothy Seow of Seow Lee Heah & Partners. The architectural language appears to be related to the imagery and illustrations, if not the underlying ideas of the Archigram Group. The 37-storey tower of Pearl Bank Apartments (1976) was an astonishingly experimental housing project by Archynamics Architects/ Archurban Architects Planners. At the time it was the tallest residential block in Singapore and had the largest number of apartments contained in a single block. The architect, Tan Cheng Siong, followed it up with another remarkable project, Pandan Valley Condominium (1976–1979). The 17-storey PUB Headquarters (1977) in Somerset Road was the result of another competition, won by AA graduate Ong Chin Bee and Tay Puay Huat of Group 2 Architects. It has a strong form, with Corbusian antecedents.

In the ten years after independence, the embryonic Singapore architectural profession was beginning to make headway and a strong portfolio of experimental architecture was emerging, driven by the enthusiasm of a small number of dedicated young architects. But this burst of innovation by the emerging Singapore practices was effectively undermined by the introduction by the Government of the Land Sales Policy. It was to have a far-reaching side effect on the development of the local profession, which was not entirely predictable.

1975: AN ARCHITECTURAL WATERSHED

The appointment of the Chinese-American architect IM Pei as the designer of the OCBC Centre (1975), in association with local firm BEP Akitek, signalled the start of a trend towards hiring foreign designers for major projects by Government departments and developers. Foreign architects, in association with a local practice, subsequently designed many prominent buildings. Moshe Safdie,

Kenzo Tange, John Portman, Paul Rudolph, Kisho Kurokawa and Hugh Stubbins were among the first wave of so-called 'signature architects'.

The reason for this influx of famous names was the introduction of the Government's Land Sales Policy introduced in 1967, as part of a strategy for the comprehensive development of the central area. Developers proposals were submitted to the Urban Renewal Department of the HDB (the forerunner of the URA), and a key factor in winning bids appears to have been the choice of internationally acclaimed architects to head the design team, with a local practice as signatories of the drawings with responsibility for compliance with local regulations and contract documentation.

Some of the resulting buildings were good examples of corporate Modernism. The OCBC Centre, the result of the Second URA Sale of Sites in 1968, exuded, "a sense of strength and permanence".[27] I M Pei, in association with Architects 61, was also the designer of Raffles City (1984–1985), a development that occupies a whole city block. It has been described as a 'city within a city'.

John Portman and Associates, in association with BEP Akitek, were responsible for the design of The Pavilion Intercontinental Hotel (1982–1983), since renamed The Regent Hotel in 1988. It was Portman's first commission for a hotel outside the USA, and the first use of an internal atrium in Singapore. Portman was later responsible, in association with DP Architects, for the design of Marina Square (1984–1985), a hotel, shopping and entertainment complex which was based on North American models. At the time it was the largest development of its kind in Southeast Asia. It had three international hotels, Pan-Pacific, Marina Mandarin and The Oriental, all utilising the Portman trademark – the internal atrium, first developed by the architect for the Peachtree development in Atlanta, USA.

Habitat at Ardmore Park (1984–1986) designed by Moshe Safdie, in association with Regional Development Consortium, was a geometric composition of interlocking cubes that resembled the Habitat project designed by Safdie for the Montreal Expo '67.

The huge influx of foreign expertise continued with the appointment of the US architect Paul Rudolph for the design of The Colonnade (1985), a 28-storey apartment block expressed as cubes stacked upon tall circular reinforced-concrete columns. The Colonnade was the first of two projects in Singapore designed by Rudolph, the other being The Concourse (1994).

The Singapore Indoor Stadium (1990) designed by Kenzo Tange, in association with RSP Architects Planners and Engineers, had much in common with the expressive framed structures that we associate with earlier sports venues designed by the Japanese architect. Tange was also brought in as design consultant on the UOB Plaza (1993–1995), the OUB Centre (1991) and UE Square (1997).

The desire of Singapore's political rulers to express progress and modernity was reflected in these international symbols of Modern corporate architecture. But there was a downside to this. "The large scale introduction of International Style buildings, may provide a superficial image of progress and modernity," noted William SW Lim at a UIA conference in the UK in 1987, "However it often destroys the fragile experiment in the evolutionary development of localism and identity."[28] This point was echoed by Tay Kheng Soon at another 1987 conference, "Foreign expertise has not broken any new ground. No new design issues or themes intrinsic to Singapore have emerged. Moreover, the designs are conceptually conventional and conservative. They have not addressed any Singapore issues."[29] As a result, the development of the nascent architectural profession in Singapore was held back from the mid 1970s onwards. It would only begin to regain momentum in the late 1990s. The largest Singapore firms such as RSP Architects, Planners and Engineers Pte Ltd; Architects 61 Pte Ltd; DP Architects Pte Ltd; SAA Architects Pte Ltd; and RDC Architects Pte Ltd were perceived, perhaps unfairly, as simply the production end of the process, with creative design being done in the USA, Japan, the UK and Australia. But the Singapore Government was pragmatic in its response to the concerns of the profession. In 1991, at the Singapore Institute of Architects annual dinner, the then Minister of State for National Development, Dr Lim Boon Yang, still maintained that, "Singapore will be better off judiciously tapping the experience, expertise and creativity of selected internationally recognised architects."

Tay Kheng Soon was also critical of the fact that the volume of work allocated to public sector architects of the HDB, PWD and Jurong Town Corporation (JTC) was seven times the volume undertaken by architects in private practice. "So long as designs and developments (of housing) are identified with the single agency," he wrote, "no real alternatives are possible."[30]

1950–1951

Nassim Hill Apartments

Nassim Hill

Architect // KA Brundle: Chief Architect Public Works Department

These three blocks of four-storey walk-up apartments were designed for senior Civil Servants soon after the end of World War II. Constructed with a reinforced concrete frame with brick infill, the walls were plastered and painted white. The planar walls are combined with horizontal fenestration and the small circular windows favoured by architects of the Modern Movement. The apartments were perfectly adapted for the tropical climate with tall rooms, deep balconies and excellent cross ventilation. The building was typical of the Modern Movement, and similarities can be seen to the work of Modernists in England such as Maxwell Fry and FRS Yorke.

1936 – 1954

Tiong Bahru Housing Estate

Tiong Bahru Road, Kim Poh Road, Guan Chuan Street, Tiong Poh Street and Eng Hoon Street.

Architect // Singapore Improvement Trust

The Singapore Improvement Trust was formed in 1927, and operated until February 1960 when the Housing and Development Board was set up. Much of Modern architecture in the early 20th Century was concerned with creating affordable housing for workers. The young architects of the SIT in Singapore were obviously aware of these developments in Europe, and the Tiong Bahru Estate was designed in the spirit and style of its European precedents. The architectural language of Singapore's first mass housing schemes included planar white walls, horizontal windows, curved stair towers and excellent natural ventilation. Limited powers and lack of funds severely restricted the effectiveness of the SIT and it was only able to house half of the population increase in the period 1947 – 1959.

1954

Asia Insurance Building

Finlayson Green

Architect // Ng Keng Siang

The post-war period saw a number of young Singaporean architects returning after their education in Australia, England and the United States. Ng Keng Siang was trained at the Bartlett School of Architecture in London and was familiar with the Modern Movement. He was the first Singaporean to become a member of the Royal Institute of British Architects. In the mid-1950s the Asia Insurance Building, designed by Ng, was the tallest building in Singapore and it can be seen as the first local attempt to produce Regional Modern architecture. The building has a tall corner tower, and the floor slabs project to create horizontal sunshading. It has survived as a landmark in spite of the unremitting pressure for redevelopment of the Central Business District.

1953–1954

Bank of China Building

Battery Road/Flint Street

Architect // CO Middlemiss of Palmer and Turner

Palmer and Turner were one of the most prominent commercial practices in Asia immediately before World War II. They set up an office in Shanghai, and came to Singapore via Hong Kong. The 18-storey Bank of China Building was amongst the first high-rise tower blocks in the region, although it is modest compared with those of today. It was a forerunner of the technology packed office blocks of the 21st Century, as it was the first centrally air-conditioned skyscraper on the island. There is an interesting duality between the early Modernist façade and the Chinese details in stone and bronze designed by craftsmen from Shanghai. Cavelieri Rodolfo Noli is credited with the design of the bank doors.

1961

The Church of the Blessed Sacrament

1 Commonwealth Avenue

Architect // Gordon Dowsett of Van Sitteran and Partners

The Church of the Blessed Sacrament reflects the Catholic religion's exploration in the 1960s of a liturgy employing a centre plan. The altar is located beneath the impressively tall space at the crossing of the short nave and the transepts. The roof takes the form of a strongly modelled reinforced concrete folded plate structure surfaced in metal 'tiles' with the underside faced in timber. The building was probably originally designed for natural ventilation now supplemented by fans and air-conditioning. Gordon Dowsett was a partner of Van Sitteran and Partners, until he moved to San Francisco in the late 1960s. Dowsett was responsible for other boldly expressive buildings such as MacPherson Road Market (1953).

1970 – 1973

Peoples Park Complex

Eu Tong Sen Street

Architect // Design Partnership

In 1967, following the break-up of Malayan Architects Co-Partnership, William Lim set up Design Partnership with Tay Kheng Soon and Koh Seow Chuan. In its first year the firm was successful with its proposal for the Peoples Park Complex, a huge mixed-use development with shops, offices and residential components. It was the first shopping centre of its type in Southeast Asia, challenging the idea of single-use zoning; the focus was two multi-storey interlocking atriums. The big 'city room' owed much to the ideas of the Metabolist Group in Japan, and when Fumihiko Maki visited the site during construction, he exclaimed "But we theorised and you people are getting it built!".

1970

Jurong Town Hall
Jurong Town Hall Road

Architect // Architects Team 3

This 1969 competition winning entry from Architects Team 3 captured the spirit of the time, and provided a symbol of Singapore's industrialisation, which was centred on Jurong Town Corporation. It appears to borrow ideas from Maekawa's Tokyo Festival Hall (1960). The building is in the form of two weighty five-storey concrete wings containing offices, between which are located a glass roofed concourse, committee rooms and a conference hall. A funnel-shaped 50-metre high clock-tower thrusts upwards at the centre of the structure. A powerful building, associated with Singapore's rapid growth to the status of a developed nation, there were many who were dismayed when its functions were relocated to a new tower block in 1999.

1974

Golden Mile Complex
Beach Road

Architect // Design Partnership

Originally named the Woh Hup Complex, the stepped profile of this mixed-use building offers the occupants of the apartments on the upper floors a panoramic view of the sea and sky. The lower floors contain offices and a retail mall. The design was intended to set the urban pattern for the development of Beach Road by employing an extruded section that would stretch along the East Coast facing the sea, serviced from the rear with a Mass Rapid Transit line and a continuous pedestrian spine. The design was influenced by the Linear City concepts of Le Corbusier and Soria y Mata. The Golden Mile Complex preceded by several years avant-garde stepped-section buildings which were built in the UK and Europe.

1975

OCBC Tower
Chulia Street

Architect // IM Pei and Partners in association with BEP Akitek

The OCBC tower, headquarters of the Overseas Chinese Banking Corporation, is a powerful statement of corporate power. Some observers see its architectural form as a representation of a giant calculator, others read it as the Chinese character for the surname of IM Pei. The building is significant for other reasons – it can be seen as marking a watershed. The appointment of the Chinese-American IM Pei as architect of the building, which resulted from the URA 2nd Sale of Sites Programme, signalled the start of a trend towards hiring foreign architects for major projects. The unintended consequence was that the development of the design potential of the nascent architectural profession in Singapore was hampered from the mid 1970s for the next two decades.

1973–1976

Futura Apartments
Leonie Hill Road

Architect // Seow Lee Heah & Partners, continued by Timothy Seow & Partners

This 25-storey apartment development consists of 69 luxury apartments and three roof-top penthouses. The façade consists of three vertical rows of oval living spaces contrasting with the circular lift cores. The architectural language is expressive with balconies that employ flying saucer-like shapes, vertical circulation reminiscent of rocket tubes, and apartment windows that appear to draw on control towers as their precedent. The language seems to be related to the imagery and illustrations, if not the underlying ideas, of Peter Cook, Ron Herron and Warren Chalk of the Archigram group in the UK, and of the Metabolists in Japan, who were active from the late 1950s until the early 1970s.

1976

Pearl Bank Apartments

Pearl Hill Road

Architect // Archynamics Architects (continued by Archurban Architects Planners)

This 38-storey tower in the form of a 3/4 cylinder was an astonishingly experimental housing project by a young Singaporean practice. At the time it was the tallest residential block in Singapore, and had the largest number of apartments contained in a single block. The structural concept utilized 10 radiating shear walls as party walls. Designed for a total occupancy of 1500 persons, it also had the highest density of any private modern residential block (1,853 persons/ha). The apartments varied from one to four bedrooms and there were eight penthouses. The 28th floor was allocated for community use. Started by Archynamics Architects, the project was completed by Archurban Architects Planners, headed by a talented designer, Tan Cheng Siong.

1971–1977

Singapore Power Building

formerly the Public Utilities Board Building

Somerset Road / Devonshire Road

Architects // Group 2 Architects

The 17-storey Public Utilities Board (PUB) Building was the result of a 1971 competition won by Ong Chin Bee and Tay Puay Huat, the partners in Group 2 Architects. It has a strong form that has been compared with Boston City Hall and with Le Corbusier's La Tourette monastery (1957–1960), though it lacks the forceful genius of Corbusier and its internal spaces are less powerful. The cantilevered upper floors and recessed lower floors combined with deep recessed windows were a logical solution to the tropical climate. Further attention to design in the tropics was provided with a generous shaded ground floor open-to-sky concourse, and a swimming pool on the roof.

1973 – 1979

Pandan Valley Condominium

Ulu Pandan Road

Architect // Archurban Architects Planners

Tan Cheng Siong was one of the most innovative architects of the 1970s. Following on from the Pearl Bank Apartments, this is another imaginative housing solution constructed in reinforced concrete and facing brick. Tan created a wide variety of apartment configurations in two point blocks, three meandering slab blocks and a series of blocks that step down both sides of a narrow valley in the manner of a hill town. He introduced scissor-section apartments, lightwells and courtyards, 'gardens in the sky', roof terraces and stepped streets. At the heart of the development are a small supermarket, a swimming pool, a gym, cafés and medical and dental facilities. By the early years of the 21st Century, Archurban Architects Planners had established an office in the Peoples Republic of China.

1983

The Regent Hotel
Tomlinson Road

Architect // John Portman & Associates in association with BEP Akitek

The practice of hiring foreign architects as design consultants became more widespread after IM Pei was employed on the OCBC Tower. Developers saw it as a means of ensuring that their bids would be successful in the URA Sale of Sites programme. The Pavilion Inter-continental (now called The Regent Hotel) was the result of the 6th Sale of Sites in 1977. It was the first hotel which John Portman designed outside the USA, and it is the first use of an internal atrium in Singapore. The atrium is 13-storeys high and is enclosed by nine sloping storeys of luxury rooms and four storeys of public rooms, between two 14-storey slab blocks. The internal space is exhilarating, although we now question the environmental responsibility of such huge air-conditioned spaces.

1983

Unit 8
71 Holland Road

Architect // William Lim Associates

The 'Pink Building', as it was often referred to in the mid-1980s, marked a watershed in the architecture of William Lim Siew Wai. Two years earlier he had quit DP Architects, the firm he had founded (as Design Partnership) in 1975, as he became increasingly disillusioned by the built results of Modernism. Unit 8 evoked extreme reactions that were partly to do with its colour, which was in sharp contrast to its more sedate neighbours. It provoked discussions about the appropriateness of its PostModern architectural language, and the contradictions and complex meanings in its form. Lim regards this project as the climax of his experiments with breaking the rules of Modernism.

1985

The Colonnade
Grange Road

Architect // Paul Rudolph in association with Archiplan Team

This 28-storey apartment block is one of two projects in Singapore designed by the acclaimed US architect Paul Rudolph (the other is the Concourse in Beach Road). The Colonnade consists of two and three-bedroom apartments sharply expressed as white and beige cubes stacked upon tall circular reinforced-concrete columns, forming an imposing six-storey high shaded void at ground level. The tall columns are a feature of several buildings by Rudolph in the USA. The structure is articulated with remarkable clarity, and the result is a powerful and elegant solution to this high-rise typology. The use of wide overhangs, external balconies and solar shading suggests an appropriate aesthetic for the tropics.

1985

Parkway Centre
formerly Parkway Builders Centre
Marine Parade Road

Architect // Akitek Tenggara

This 13-storey L-shaped office block encompasses a soaring naturally ventilated atrium enclosed in a glass-clad, aluminium tube space frame. From the mid-1960s, architect Tay Kheng Soon of Akitek Tenggara argued the need for imported architectural models to be carefully reassessed in terms of their climatic and cultural suitability. This is Akitek Tenggara's riposte to the ubiquitous enclosed atrium, which had originated 30 degrees north of the equator in Atlanta, Georgia. Tay Kheng Soon's design is glazed on two sides with a series of giant louvres that draw air upwards and naturally ventilate the atrium space. There is thus an attempt to use the tropical climate positively and to create sustainable architecture.

1984–1985

Raffles City
Bras Basah Road/Beach Road

Architect // IM Pei in association with Architects 61

Raffles City occupies a complete city block, and at the time of its completion included the tallest hotel tower in the world. It has been described as a 'city within a city', with three hotels grouped around a huge internal atrium the size of a substantial outdoor urban square. One of the most fascinating features of this internal city courtyard was its 'glass bridge', though this was subsequently removed. Initially the tallest of the three hotel towers dominated the city centre, but is now rivalled by other skyscrapers in the CBD and no longer seems so overpowering. All three towers are faced in silver aluminium cladding. The Compass Rose restaurant on the penthouse floor provides unique views of the island of Singapore.

1984 – 1986

Habitat Ardmore Park

Ardmore Park

Architect // Moshe Safdie in association with Regional Development Consortium (RDC Architects)

This residential development borrows unashamedly from the Habitat building constructed for the Montreal Expo '67, which was also designed by Moshe Safdie. The original was an experiment in prefabrication of complete apartment units, which were then lifted and slotted into place in a complex matrix. The Habitat at Ardmore Park is also a controlled geometric composition of interlocking cubes, although it does not employ the prefabrication techniques used in Montreal. The apartments have landscaped, sheltered outdoor rooms carved out of the solid form, which are particularly appropriate for the tropical climate.

1989

Tampines North Community Centre

Tampines Street 41/Avenue 7

Architect // William Lim Associates

Tampines North Community Centre was a seminal building, which redefined the role of a community centre in the Singapore context. The building can be read as a metaphor for Singapore society in the late 1980s. The encompassing perimeter wall can be seen as the strongly ordered social structure, and within the perimeter wall a variety of elements and value systems are expressed as individual fragments. Like the society they mirror, the fragments sometimes burst out of the ordered constraints; more frequently they can be observed in harmonious relationships within the structured geometry of the complex.

1990

Singapore Indoor Stadium

2 Stadium Road

Architect // RSP Architects Planners and Engineers in association with Kenzo Tange

The Singapore Indoor Stadium has much in common with the expressive framed structures that we have come to associate with earlier sports venues designed by the Japanese Master Architect Kenzo Tange. His most famous work is arguably the Tokyo Olympic Pool (1964). The Singapore Indoor Stadium is symmetrical with a diamond shaped plan. The roof is the dominant feature, and the shiny metal clad surface lightly angles upwards above the heavy concrete plinth. It has an unsupported span of 100 metres and rises to a peak of 40 metres. It has evoked subliminal associations with the roof of a Chinese temple and with Mount Fuji.

1991–2003 // ARCHITECTURE AND THE GLOBAL CITY

In 1990 Lee Kuan Yew handed over the reins of government to Goh Chok Tong and the 'second generation' leaders. It was a smooth transition intended to continue successful economic and social policies, and to demonstrate the country's stability in a sometimes volatile region.

Singapore was increasingly tied into the global economy, and foreign architects continued to be widely employed as design consultants by both government and private clients on many large and prestigious commissions. The Hitachi Towers/Caltex House complex (1993) at Collyer Quay, designed by Murphy Jahn Architects in association with Architects 61, was a conspicuously well-crafted corporate building. UOB Plaza (1993–1995) in Raffles Place, by Kenzo Tange Associates and Architects 61, demonstrates the manipulation of a simple geometric form. Kenzo Tange also designed the UE Square Development in association with Architects 61 Pte Ltd.

The seven-storey steel-and-glass cone, which acts as a dramatic entrance to Wheelock Place (1994) from Orchard Road, is a trademark of the eminent Japanese architect Kisho Kurokawa who was the design consultant, working with Wong and Ouyang, and RSP Architects Planners and Engineers for this retail and office complex.

Temasek Polytechnic (1995) was the last major built project of the renowned British architect James Stirling, who worked in association with DP Architects Pte Ltd. DP Architects also provided support services for Mitchell Giurgola and Thorp Associates on the Singapore Discovery Centre (1996). An increasing number of foreign architects were commissioned in the late 1990s. Singapore's Marina Centre has been dubbed 'Little America' as a result of the proliferation of buildings designed by American architects and its conspicuously American urban spaces.[31] Millenia Tower (1996), designed by Kevin Roche, John Dinkeloo and Associates, is the centrepiece of the Pontiac Marina development, which includes the Ritz Carlton Millenia (1996) by Kevin Roche of Connecticut and the Conrad International (1997) designed by John Burgee of New York. Millenia Walk (1996) was designed by Philip Johnson, while the convention centre at Suntec City (1994) is the work of the New York practice of Tsao and McKown. The urban spaces speak of corporate power.

Dominic Perrault was the design consultant for the neatly designed, though climatically inappropriately orientated, Alliance Française de Singapour. Philip Cox of Australia was the design architect of the Singapore Expo 2000 Pavilion, and Arquitectonica, from Florida, have contributed two apartment blocks remarkable only for their banality.

AN ARCHITECTURE OF RESISTANCE

Several local practices resisted the trend towards working in association with foreign firms. The result was that they were generally denied the chance to work on large projects, but as a consequence they became more critical designers. The issues of identity and critical regionalism entered the architectural discourse in the mid-1980s, even though they were debated by a relatively small group of architects and academics.

Tay Kheng Soon, of Akitek Tenggara, argued the need for imported architectural models to be carefully reassessed in terms of their climatic and cultural suitability. Parkway Builders Centre (1985) in Marine Parade Road was Tay's riposte to the ubiquitous enclosed atrium which had originated 30 degrees north of the equator in Atlanta, Georgia. There was an attempt to use the tropical climate positively and to create sustainable architecture. Akitek Tenggara's design for the Institute of Technical Education at Bishan (1986) continued Tay's exploration of a modern architectural language for the tropics. Tay raised critical questions about the direction of architecture in Singapore. The enormous reliance on air conditioning and the uncritical acceptance of imported models were interrogated. With the King Albert Park House (1994) a client, who was sympathetic to the architect's ideas on 'green' architecture, gave Tay an opportunity to define a tropical lifestyle. Tay Kheng

Soon was able to pursue these ideas on a modern tropical architectural language in the Kadang Kerbau Hospital (1997). The building took the notion of a language of "Line, Edge, Mesh and Shade" to a new level of sophistication.[32]

William Lim Associates have fulfilled a similar role; their architecture constantly questioned accepted norms. Tampines North Community Centre (1989) was a seminal building, which redefined the role of a community centre in the Singapore context. The Reuters House (1990) critically addresses the issue of a Contemporary Vernacular architecture and how to be "modern yet rooted in one's own culture". The concept of community was again addressed in the Marine Parade Community Centre (2000).

Tang Guan Bee has danced to a different tune throughout his career. Sometimes referred to as the 'oldest young architect in Singapore', from the inception of his practice Tang Guan Bee has been acknowledged as the most avant-garde of Singapore architects. He produced a number of remarkable projects throughout the 1980s and 1990s, often on the tightest of budgets, such as the Eastpoint Shopping Centre (1996), which stands out as a significant counterpoint to the often sanitised and themed environments of the modern shopping mall. The Windsor Park House (1997), by Tangguanbee Architects is a reflection of many aspects of contemporary culture.

Chan Sau Yan of CSYA Architects produces pragmatic yet elegant architectural solutions. Both his Nassim Jade (1997) with poetic curved copper roofs, and Bournemouth 8 (1998) which experiments with the notion of a small high-density community, achieve a sense of privacy in a increasingly densely populated island.

Apart from these local practices and a handful of others, much of the architecture of the 1980s and early 1990s was anonymous corporate stuff churned out at great speed in a period of almost continuous economic growth. There was little time for reflection on the heritage that was being sacrificed in the process, or on the quality of the urban spaces that were being produced.

The mid-1980s brought a realisation that much of the built heritage had been already torn down in the urban renewal process. Many valuable old buildings had been lost, and concerned individuals began to voice disquiet. Lee Kip Lin wrote a number of books that highlighted the value of memory, including 'Emerald Hill' in 1984.[33]

Another book, 'Pastel Portraits' by Gretchen Liu,[34] highlighted the remarkable beauty of the surviving heritage. In 1986 the Singapore Heritage Society was registered. In 1988 the Ministry of National Development designated four conservation areas, and at the same time Rent Decontrol was introduced in the designated areas.

THE EXPATRIATE ARCHITECT

For over a century, expatriate architects have come to Singapore, attracted by its stable business environment, and put down roots. More importantly they have contributed to the local design culture. The Australian architect Kerry Hill set up Kerry Hill Architects in 1979 and operates his international practice from the city-state. Hill has built up an international reputation designing mainly, though not exclusively, resort hotels. With Genesis (1994–1997), a five-storey mixed-use development with commercial office space topped by apartments, Hill raised critical questions about the integration of tradition with modern technology. More recently the Singapore Cricket Association Cricket Pavilion (1999) is a further development of an architectural language which affirms Hill's roots in Modernism while expressing the wisdom of Asian precedents in the tropical context.

Argentine-born Ernesto Bedmar arrived in Singapore in 1984. His Eu House I (1994) was seminal, raising questions about the erasure of local identity in Singapore's architecture. Almost a decade later at Trevose Crescent (2002) Bedmar has produced a stunning interpretation of Tropical Modern architecture which synthesises the bungalow typology with the townhouse typology.

Penang-born Chan Soo Khian set up the practice of SCDA Architects in 1995, and his Coronation Road West House (1998–2000) is typical of the practice's residential work. The interior has been crafted employing planes, surfaces, voids and light to produce multiple spatial experiences. The Lincoln Modern (2003) by SCDA is a 30-storey condominium in the form of 56 split-level, apartments, studios and penthouses. The architectural language emphasises elegant transparency in the manner of Mies van der Rohe's Lake Shore Drive Apartments, designed in 1948.

Singapore has, as a Global City, become a hub from which these architects and others operate in markets throughout Asia and further afield.

1995: THE NEXT GENERATION

Foreign architects will inevitably continue to contribute to the architectural culture in Singapore, as the island is so intrinsically locked into the global economy. At the beginning of the 21st Century, projects designed by Richard Meier, Michael Wilford and Norman Foster were completed. Others, including the National Library Building (designed by Malaysian Ken Yeang), North One (master-planned by Iraq-born, London-based Zaha Hadid) and the Supreme Court Building (designed by Norman Foster from the UK), are on site. Meier, the design consultant for the Camden Medical Centre (2000) was a member of the famed 'New York Five'. The project is an elegant 18-storey cylindrical tower that resembles earlier Meier designs, most notably the Madison Square Garden Redevelopment in 1987. The breathtakingly beautiful Expo MRT Station (2001) was Norman Foster's first project in Singapore, and exhibits a grandeur unequalled in any other MRT station on the island. The Supreme Court Building designed by Foster is scheduled for completion in 2005. The Esplanade-Theatres on the Bay (2002), a collaboration between DP Architects Pte Ltd and British architect Michael Wilford, provoked a significant backlash against the practice of employing foreign design consultants on significant cultural icons when models were revealed in 1994.

A new National Trades Union Congress Headquarters is progressing on site, designed by the New York based practice of Kohn Pederson Fox. British architects RMJM are the design consultants for a new Polytechnic, Will Alsop from the UK is working on a project in Clarke Quay, and Fumihiko Maki from Japan is involved on another project, while Kisho Kurokawa, no stranger to Singapore, is designing a large ferris wheel intended to surpass the London Eye.

But while established international design practices continue to attract the attention of the architectural media, a younger generation of local architects – most of them born around the time of independence, are increasingly occupying centre stage in the city-state. Many of them set up practice in the mid 1990s and their work is comparable with the best produced anywhere in the world.

Mok Wei Wei of W Architects (formerly William Lim Associates) is one of the leading architects in this younger 'group'. In the Morley Road House (1998) by Mok Wei Wei, there is a convergence of memories and connections to cultural roots in a design that simultaneously advances the Modernist paradigm. His other recent projects include Patterson Edge (1999), The Loft (2002) and The Arris (2003). Kay Ngee Tan and Tan Teck Khiam were in partnership as KNTA Architects from 1993 to 2003. They designed a number of residential projects including Check House No.1 and Check House No.2, and in 2000 the practice (in association with Edward Cullinen) won an international competition for the design of the new Singapore Management University (SMU). Wong Mun Summ set up in partnership with Richard Hassell, an Australian, as WOHA Architects in 1994. With their Victoria Park Houses (2000) they produced three dwelling configurations from a basic plan type – a combination of poetry and pragmatism that pervades all their work. In 1999 WOHA were the winners of another international competition for the design of two major MRT stations, to be completed in 2005. They also completed a striking residential tower, No 1 Moulmein Rise in 2003. There is a critical mass of these new practices including MAPS Design Studio, FORUM Architects, MKPL Architects, HYLA Architects, and LOOK Architects. Add to them a still younger group which includes K2LD Architects and HAM Architects. On the endeavours of this generation of design-orientated practices (together with CSDA Architects, Bedmar and Shi Design, CSYA Architects and Tangguanbee Architects) hangs the future of the built environment in Singapore.

A cool Modernism has come to characterize the work of several of these architects. There is a fascination with prismatic boxes and with the exquisite detailing of metal and glass.[35] On the surface there is a remarkable similarity about some of the resultant works, although subtle differences are revealed if one closely interrogates the intentions and the response to programme. Each of these architects, in their own way, is searching for a personal response to climate and culture, and to the integration of Modernism and tradition.

For 140 years Singapore was governed by Great Britain. There is an understandable dismay among some architects that, having fought so hard for her independence 40 years ago, the island is now drawn into a relationship with a global economy that promotes a new form of colonisation whereby architecture must genuflect to Western taste. There is a deep-seated resentment that so many major projects since 1975 have been awarded to foreign practices. It is a trend which is accompanied by the tendency for local architects to emulate uncritically the architectural language of the West.

Singapore architecture is at a critical juncture as it plots a course into the 21st Century.

1993

Hitachi Tower / Caltex House

16 Collyer Quay / 30 Raffles Place

Architect // Murphy Jahn Architects in association with Architects 61 Pte Ltd

The Hitachi Tower/Caltex House complex is a conspicuously well-crafted corporate building clad in steel, aluminium and glass. Hitachi Tower provides a strong visual image when seen from the East Coast Parkway, while the tower of Caltex House acts as a counterpoint to the OUB Tower on Raffles Place. The two towers are significant for the manner in which they address the site imperatives and stitch together the city fabric as part of the evolving urban design of the Central Business District. A naturally ventilated arcade cuts through the podium of the two towers linking Raffles Place to Collyer Quay. For older Singaporeans it preserves a memory of the historic Change Alley which formerly existed on this site.

1993–1994

Eu House I
Belmont Road

Architect // Ernesto Bedmar of Bedmar and Shi Designers Pte Ltd

The Eu House consists of a group of four pavilions around a pool. The influences upon the Argentine-born designer of the house are elusive, but there are unquestionably references to Chinese culture in the entrance foyer, the hierarchy of privacy and the grouping of the pavilions around a courtyard. The open volumes of the rooms evoke the Thai *sala*, while there are also memories of Malaccan *kampong* houses. All of these have cultural relevance in Singapore, which is a multicultural society of migrants from many parts of Asia. Ernesto Bedmar, who has lived in Singapore for two decades, has integrated the various cultural influences in an unselfconscious manner.

1994

The Concourse
298/300 Beach Road

Architect // Paul Rudolph Architects in association with Architects 61 Pte Ltd

Approaching the city from Changi Airport, the 41-storey tower of the Concourse stands out as a landmark with its distinctive silhouette viewed across the Kallang River basin. The conspicuous architectural feature is the aluminium curtain walling system incorporating inclined windows which form clusters of units. These clusters are stacked (like dinner plates) one above the other, rotating around the building. The octagonal tower is supported on huge *pilotti* similar to other Rudolph Buildings such as the Art and Architecture Building at Yale University (1964). At the base of the tower are a three-story retail podium and nine storeys of serviced apartments. It is an interesting programme that critically questions the Modernist practice of single use zoning.

1992–1994

King Albert Park House

King Albert Park

Architect // Tay Kheng Soon of Akitek Tenggara II

A superb site and a client who was sympathetic to the architect's intentions to explore ideas on 'green' architecture gave Tay Kheng Soon an opportunity to define a tropical lifestyle. The house has all the attributes of a well designed house in the tropics - major living spaces that are open-to-sky, orientation to catch the prevailing breezes, openness in the plan arrangement to encourage cross-ventilation, extensive use of water and planting, wide overhanging eaves, secondary shading devices and the restriction of air-conditioning only to rooms where it is strictly necessary. The architectural language employed is uncompromisingly Modern, with thin projecting concrete slab edges, light diffusing screens and a raised undercroft providing shade.

1994

Tampines New Town

Tampines New Town

Architect // Housing and Development Board

The Housing and Development Board was set up in 1960, and today almost 90 percent of the Singapore population live in high-rise public housing. Once out of the city centre this is the dominant image in the landscape. Tampines New Town serves not only the immediate population, but the whole north-east sector of the island. The New Town is divided into eight neighbourhoods, each with between 5,000 and 6,000 apartments. Within each neighbourhood, a centre with retail shops, eating places and markets is located within a ten-minute walking distance of all apartments. Each neighbourhood is further divided into precincts of four to eight housing blocks.

1994

Wheelock Place

Orchard Road / Scotts Road

Architect // Kisho Kurokawa in association with Wong and Ouyang, and RSP Architects Planners and Engineers

The seven-storey steel-and-glass cone, which acts as the dramatic entrance to Wheelock Place from Orchard Road, is a major landmark in the tourist and retail belt. The cone is a trademark of the eminent Japanese architect Kisho Kurokawa, who was the design consultant for this retail and office complex. The 16-storey office tower is clad in blue-tinted glass and capped by an aluminium cone. A colonnaded pedestrian walkway is incorporated around the building to link it to the Orchard Road mall. An underpass links the building directly to the MRT and forms part of the Orchard Road underground pedestrian network.

1993–1995

UOB Plaza
80 Raffles Place

Architect // Kenzo Tange Associates (Concept and Master Planner) in association with Architects 61 Pte Ltd

UOB Plaza demonstrates the manipulation of a simple geometric form to create a visually exciting landmark office building, which symbolises Singapore's emergence as a global centre for finance and banking. The complex comprises two octagonal towers linked by an office bridge that spans a 12-metre high public plaza. The two towers are composed of octagonal plans juxtaposed at 45-degree angles to each other, and they are superimposed in a series of geometrical rotations. The curtain wall system is a state-of-the-art thin-skin performance wall envelope of white and grey granite, aluminium framing and insulated grey glass. UOB Plaza terminates a row of restored shophouses along South Boat Quay. This is one of five high-profile buildings in Singapore conceptualised by the renowned Japanese architect Kenzo Tange.

1995

Temasek Polytechnic

21 Tampines Avenue 1

Architect // James Stirling Michael Wilford and Associates in association with DP Architects Pte Ltd

Temasek Polytechnic was the last major built project of the renowned British architect James Stirling, who worked in partnership with Michael Wilford. A strong sense of unity exists in the architectural forms and spaces, and Stirling's preoccupation with formal geometry and coherent circulation is evident. At the centre of the project is a horseshoe shaped library and administrative block embracing a central plaza, approached by a ceremonial ramp and stairs. It is a brilliantly successful 'urban' space that encourages social communication and interaction among staff and students. The use of a limited palette of materials assists in the legibility of the composition.

1996

Eastpoint Shopping Centre

Simei Street, Simei

Architect // Tang Guan Bee of Tangguanbee Architects

Eastpoint Shopping Centre stands out as a significant counterpoint to the often sanitised and themed environments of the modern shopping mall. Ordinary industrial materials and details are employed, and there is a noticeable absence of fastidious details and designer finishes. Tang Guan Bee intentionally erases the exclusive image of more up-market shopping developments, and consequently Eastpoint is accessible to a broad range of people. It has a carnival-like atmosphere that recalls the Great World and Beauty World shopping bazaars that flourished in Singapore in the 1960s and 1970s. The overall ambience epitomises the complexity, imperfections and anonymity of the contemporary city.

1996

Millenia Tower

1 Temasek Avenue

Architect // Kevin Roche, John Dinkeloo and Associates in association with DP Architects Pte Ltd

Millenia Tower is the centrepiece of the Pontiac Marina development. The tower is 41 storeys tall and exudes a powerful presence. The scale is monumental; a monolithic square shaft rises from four huge cylindrical volumes at the base and is capped by a theatrically illuminated skeletal pyramid top. The lobby boasts an entire wall covered with a painting by Frank Stella. Kevin Roche is one of a several internationally acclaimed architects employed as design consultant by the developer of this site. The nearby Ritz Carlton Millenia Hotel (1996) was also conceptualised by Kevin Roche, John Dinkeloo and Partners, and the adjoining shopping mall – Millenia Walk (1996) – was designed by Philip Johnson and John Burgee Architects.

1996

Check House I

Cluny Road

Architect // Tan Kay Ngee and Tan Teck Kiam of KNTA Architects

There is a faintly nautical air about Check House I with circular windows in the elevation facing the entrance drive. In the Singapore context, this was a seminal house when completed in 1996, for it was the first major built work of the unconventional practice of KNTA, comprising Tan Teck Kiam and Tan Kay Ngee, the latter a winner of the prestigious RIBA International Student Prize. The design broke away from the then current obsession with questions of regionalism, identity and tropicality. It suggested alternative ways of looking at residential architecture in the tropics, which widened the debate into methods of transforming and translating the vernacular. Whether the architecture is a successful climatic response is uncertain, but the house is certainly a beautiful object.

1994–1997

Genesis
170 Bukit Timah Road

Architect // Kerry Hill Architects

The Australian architect Kerry Hill set up practice in Singapore in 1979. He has subsequently built up an international reputation designing mainly, though not exclusively, resort hotels. Here he turns his hand to a five-storey mixed use development with commercial office space topped by apartments. The building has an enigmatic quality as both plate glass façades are screened by veils of fine *balau* timber louvres. The detached timber screen allows light to penetrate into the building while simultaneously providing privacy and protection from direct sun and rain. The building is a fine example of integrating tradition with modern technology. It has a refinement and delicacy normally associated with smaller scale objects.

1997

Nassim Jade
Nassim Road

Architect // Chan Sau Yan of CSYA Architects

Given the pressure on land in Singapore, which pushes the prospect of owning a landed property beyond the reach of all but 10% of the population, the aspiration of most Singaporeans is to own an apartment in a condominium. Nassim Jade accommodates 39 units together with a private swimming pool, gymnasium, and spa and function room on a 10,000 square metre site formerly occupied by Jade House, 'Tiger Balm King' Au Boon Haw's villa. The architectural language is notable for the curved geometric form of the copper clad roofs (a distinctive way of complying with building regulations) and the system of adjustable folding/sliding timber panels that were devised as a permeable skin.

1997

Windsor Park House
Windsor Park

Architect // Tang Guan Bee of
Tangguanbee Architects

From the inception of his practice in the 1980s Tang Guan Bee has long been acknowledged as the most avant-garde of Singapore architects. Viewed from afar the Windsor Park House, designed for a film director, stands out from its conventional neighbours with its sail-like roof, transparent walls, primary colours and copper-clad pavilions. The house is a reflection of many aspects of contemporary culture, a desire to be visible yet anonymous, to express difference yet yearn for solitude, and to live in the public arena yet retain a private self. The apparent contradictions and chaos achieve a unity through a strong conceptual framework and an underlying tension that holds the fragments together.

1988 – 1997

Kadang Kerbau Hospital

Kampong Java Road / Bukit Timah Road

Architect // Tay Kheng Soon of Akitek Tenggara II in association with the Public Works Department

Akitek Tenggara II won the commission for the design of the Kadang Kerbau Hospital for Women and Children in a 1988 competition. Legibility was a prime concern, and a centralised core placed on the axis of the building efficiently connects the two functions of the hospital. There are separate entrances for ambulant and non-ambulant patients. The plan and section of the building advanced Tay Kheng Soon's ideas on Modern Tropical architecture as an "architecture of Line, Edge, Mesh and Shade". This is evident in the use of pre-cast horizontal concrete shading louvres on the principal façades and the tapering of the podium, which achieves a gentle merging of the building with the landscape.

1998

Institute of Southeast Asian Studies

Heng Mui Keng Terrace

Architect // Public Works Department

The architectural language of the Institute of Southeast Asian Studies (ISEAS) draws heavily upon regional architectural precedents. The building has a tripartite composition consisting of a granite base or podium, concrete post and beam superstructure (analogous with timber construction) and a pitched clay tiled roof with generous overhanging eaves. The various functions of this academic think-tank revolve around a central courtyard inspired by the in-between spaces found within a traditional Balinese compound house. The architectural team of Cheah Kok Ming and Poon Hin Kong combined a number of general characteristics of Southeast Asian traditional vernacular architectures concerning form, space, materials and tectonics. The landscape is by the Balinese based Made Wijaya (Michael White).

1998

Morley Road House

4 Morley Road

Architect // Mok Wei Wei of William Lim Associates

The underlying ideas in the Morley Road House are derived from the movement and the framing of views within a Chinese garden, specifically a garden in Suchow with which Mok Wei Wei is familiar. The architectural language employed to convey the narrative is undeniably Modern: white planar surfaces are juxtaposed alongside grey granite walls and aluminium framed, clear glazed fenestration. Flat concrete roofs are supported on slender circular columns and project beyond the walls of the house. In the Morley Road House there is a convergence of memories and connections to cultural roots in a design that simultaneously advances the Modernist paradigm.

2000

Camden Medical Centre

Grange Road/Orchard Boulevard

Architect // Richard Meier Architect in association with DP Architects Pte Ltd

Richard Meier, the design consultant for the Camden Medical Centre was a member of the famed 'New York Five' along with Peter Eisenman, Michael Graves, John Hedjuk and Charles Gwathmey. The Camden Medical Centre is an elegant 18-storey cylindrical tower that resembles earlier Meier designs, most notably the Madison Square Garden Redevelopment (1987). Richard Meier's work is instantly recognisable by his trademark white panels and the systematic use of a grid that covers the plans and elevations. The architecture conveys a sense of calmness appropriate for its purpose as a hospital, although it is not the best of Meier's work, somehow lacking a real presence.

1998–2000

Coronation Road West House

178 Coronation Road West

Architect // SCDA Architects

The Coronation Road West House affirms SCDA's commitment to the language of Modern architecture. The form is a balanced composition of planes and boxes: a heavy line is inscribed across the site by a reinforced concrete wall anchored at one end by the main house, a heavy box attached to the ground. This is balanced by a smaller, lightweight, transparent box which sits atop and cantilevers out from, the other end of the wall. The fulcrum of this asymmetrical composition is the entrance lobby centrally located on the site. The assured and uncompromising design stirs memories of the interlocking volumes and planes of the early Modern architecture of the De Stijl group, notably the Schroeder House (1924) in Utrecht by G T Rietveld.

2000

Gallery Hotel
Robertson Quay

Architect // William Lim Associates and Tangguanbee Architects

Gallery Hotel was conceptualised as a HIP (Highly Individual Place) Hotel, a place for the traveller who looks for something out of the ordinary. The intention was that it should not simply be a place to stay on reaching one's destination, but that it should be the destination, the end itself. Located in an area recently cleared of riverside warehouses, the site itself is in transition, which creates an intriguing and slightly disconcerting tension. The building reads like a puzzle with a number of disparate forms collaged together, and various elements attached like body prosthetics. The making of the building was equally curious for it involved a potentially fiery collaboration between William SW Lim and Tang Guan Bee, two of Singapore's most avant-garde practitioners.

2000

Victoria Park Houses

Victoria Park

Architect // WOHA Architects

WOHA Architects have shoehorned three houses into a small irregular shaped site. They have taken Singapore's strict planning and development constraints, and utilising a mathematical diagram, they have produced three configurations from a basic plan type. Achieving privacy is a major consideration in the increasingly densely developed city-state, and WOHA have refined what they term the "upside-down house". The upper levels use careful placement of openings, together with louvred screens, to allow the house to be open, yet private. Views are directed into inner courts created by the blank walls of adjoining houses.

2000

Marine Parade Community Centre

Marine Parade Road / Still Road South

Architect // William Lim Associates

Community Centres are an integral part of Singapore life. They were first introduced by the British to combat communist subversives. They were then adopted and developed by the Government as a means of forging bonds between the disparate elements in a multi-cultural society, and were strongly tied to the place of residence. But the concept of community is changing and Marine Parade Community Centre's multiple programmes include a Starbucks Café, a 'black box' theatre and a branch library. The activities of the complex are planned to overlap and coalesce, becoming a one-stop destination for the entire family. The rich congruence of programmes is expressed by William Lim Associates as a collage of diverse elements and materials.

2001

Expo MRT Station
Changi South

Architect // Foster and Partners

Norman Foster is the acclaimed British designer of such icons as the Hong Kong and Shanghai Bank tower and the Chek Lap Kok Airport. The breathtakingly beautiful Expo MRT Station was his first project in Singapore and exhibits a grandeur unequalled in any other MRT station on the island. The titanium-clad roof is a three-dimensional curve derived from the shape of a torus, and is supported on two pairs of 'V' twin columns separated by a 70-metre span. The ticket hall at one end of the station has a circular stainless steel disc as a roof. The station is spectacular piece of engineering with an imposing presence and an awesome beauty.

2002

Trevose Crescent

Trevose Crescent

Architect // Ernesto Bedmar of Bedmar and Shi Designers Pte Ltd

At Trevose Crescent, Ernesto Bedmar has produced a stunning interpretation of Tropical Modern architecture. The site is approximately 130 metres long and falls dramatically, 14 metres, from the rear boundary to the front access road. Eleven residential units, each 26 metres deep and 6 metres wide, are arranged in a single file. A twelth unit with a slightly different configuration is located at the eastern end of the site. Each unit is separated from its neighbour by a private courtyard four metres in width, with a 10 metre long swimming pool with a glazed acrylic end overlooking the public road. Essentially, what the architect has done is to synthesise the bungalow typology (which requires a statutory minimum of four metres between dwellings) with the townhouse typology.

1994 – 2002

Esplanade – Theatres on the Bay

Raffles Avenue

Architect // DP Architects Pte Ltd in association with Michael Wilford and Partners London

The twin domes of the Esplanade-Theatres on the Bay have attracted their share of critical comments. The project, a collaboration between DP Architects Pte Ltd and British architect Michael Wilford, provoked a significant backlash (when models were revealed in 1994) against the practice of employing foreign design consultants, particularly on projects of major cultural significance. It was argued that foreign consultants were not conversant with local and regional cultural practices. Some critics have likened the spiky sunshade devices, which cover the completed 2,000-seat theatre and the 1,800-seat concert hall, to two durians. The architects argue that the patterns are evocative of geometric patterns in nature, as well as woven rattan walls in traditional Asian building forms.

2002

Tree House
23 Gallop Park

Architect // Joseph Lim Ee Mun

In amongst all the high-rise, high-density projects in Singapore it is a delight to encounter something as ephemeral as a tree-house. This is Joseph Lim's second tree-house, the first having been built in his own garden for his three sons. The branches of tropical trees in Singapore generally do not have the stability or strength to carry the live loads demanded of a tree-house, and this particular *Tembusu* tree was also the subject of a preservation order. Lim's solution was to build a lightweight steel and timber structure from two outriggers that embrace the tree and an adjoining *Jering* species, without placing loads directly on the branches. The trees have also been fitted with lightning conductors recommended by the Parks and Recreation Department.

2003

1 Moulmein Rise

Moulmein Rise

Architect // WOHA Architects

1 Moulmein Rise is a 30-storey apartment block, which arguably deserves the accolade of Singapore's most exquisitely designed high-rise building. The tower has two apartments on each floor and two penthouse suites. At the foot of the building is a 50-metre lap pool, a 25-metre pool and a wading pool in a series of stepped terraces, while the penthouse suites have private lap pools and roof terraces. Details of the project exhibit great ingenuity; one example is where traditional 'monsoon' windows have been re-interpreted to permit controlled natural ventilation. The block is orientated north-south with one elevation substantially glazed and the other clad in perforated stainless steel sheet.

2003

The Lincoln Modern
Lincoln Road

Architect // SCDA Architects

The Lincoln Modern is a 30-storey apartment block in the form of 56 split-level apartments, studios and penthouses. The residential apartments are a development of the section and plan forms first explored in Le Corbusier's two-storey prototype dwelling for the Immeubles-Villas project of 1922, which was subsequently displayed in the Esprit Nouveau Pavilion at the Paris 1925 exhibition. The interior of the Esprit Nouveau pavilion developed the idea of spatial overlaps, with the upper floor as a gallery overlooking the main living space. The architectural language of SCDA's high-rise towers, with the use of slender aluminium brise-soleil and smooth curtain walling, emphasises elegant transparency in the manner of Mies van der Rohe's seminal Lake Shore Drive Apartments, designed in 1948.

2003

The Arris
Yan Kit Road

Architect // Mok Wei Wei of
W Architects

The Arris, a ten-storey inner-city apartment block, builds upon ideas explored by Mok Wei Wei in the Paterson Edge (1999). The project combines a high degree of sophistication in its architectural language with a response to programme and site. Mok's approach is concerned with defining the perimeter of the block, and thereafter 'cutting out' space to create porosity in the form, though a trace of the perimeter is retained. Horizontal lines are emphasised and the block is stepped back at the seventh storey, where a 'hanging' lap pool and a gymnasium are located. There is a duality in the plan with a glazed façade looking east shaded by mature trees, and a complex yet dense west façade overlooking a drainage canal.

2003

Villa O
20 Hartley Grove

Architect // Tan Kok Meng and Ling Hao of HAM Architects

The final project in this short history of Singapore architecture is indicative of the ability of a talented generation of architects born at the time Singapore achieved independence – architects who are now in their late 30s or early 40s. Villa O is a remarkable house by two young architects who have designed a number of projects stimulating architectural discourse. Villa O is a rectangular three-storey house with a basement and roof terrace in what the designers call "a very personal, non-universal, un-Modern, non-reductive-rational" approach that explores spatial and tactile experience. The designers are concerned with creating a rich variety of sensory and tactile stimuli within an enclosed world. They are concerned with the experience and understanding of space rather than the contemplation of an object.

Singapore City

#	Name	#	Name	#	Name
1	South Boat Quay 1822	20	Victoria Memorial Hall and Theatre 1856–1862	39	Eden Hall - British High Commissioner's Residence 1904
2	Kampong Glam 1822	21	St Andrews Cathedral 1856–1862	40	Chesed-El Synagogue 1905
3	Chinatown 1822	22	St Josephs Institute 1865–1867	41	Central Fire Station 1909
4	Fuk Tak Ch'i Temple 1824	23	Empress Place Building 1864–1867	42	Tao Nan School 1910
5	Old Parliament House 1826–1827	24	The Istana 1867–1869	43	St George's Church, Tanglin 1911
6	Nagore Durgha Indian Muslim Shrine 1828–1830	25	Cavanagh Bridge 1868–1869	44	Madrasah Alsagoff 1912
7	Old Christian Cemetery, Fort Canning 1834	26	Tan Si Chong Su Temple 1870	45	Goodwood Hill 1920s
8	Armenian Church 1835	27	Orchard Road Presbyterian Church 1877–1878	46	The College of Medicine Building 1923–1926
9	Jamae (Chulia) Mosque 1830–1835	28	Sun Yat Sen Villa 1880	47	Great Southern Hotel 1927
10	The Istana Kampong Glam 1840	29	Singapore Cricket Club 1884	48	Sultan Mosque 1924–1928
11	Thian Hock Keng Temple 1839–1842	30	Tan Yeok Nee House 1885	49	The Fullerton Building 1919–1928
12	Sri Mariamman Temple 1843	31	Raffles Hotel 1886	50	City Hall 1926–1929
13	Little India 1844	32	National Museum 1886–1887	51	Koon Seng Road 1929
14	Hajjah Fatimah Mosque 1846	33	Thong Chai Medical Hall 1892	52	Capital Building 1929–1930
15	Cathedral of the Good Shepherd 1843–1846	34	Telok Ayer Market 1894	53	31 and 33 Club Street 1932
16	State of Johore Mosque 1849	35	Atbara 1898	54	Clifford Pier 1931–1933
17	Convent of the Holy Infant Jesus 1854	36	Goodwood Park Hotel 1900	55	23 Ridout Road 1934
18	Fort Canning 1859	37	Emerald Hill Road 1901	56	Hill Street Building 1934–1936
19	Botanic Gardens and Burkill Hall 1859	38	Jinriksha Building 1903		

Singapore City Central District

FOR MORE INFORMATION CONSULT PERIPLUS TRAVEL MAPS - SINGAPORE ISLAND AND CITY

57	Kallang Airport 1937	76	Unit 8 1983	95	Nassim Jade 1997
58	Singapore Railway Station 1932–1937	77	The Colonnade 1985	96	Windsor Park House 1997*
59	Chee Guan Chiang House 1938	78	Parkway Centre 1985	97	Kadang Kerbau Hospital 1988–1997
60	The Supreme Court 1937–1939	79	Raffles City 1984–85	98	Institute of Southeast Asian Studies 1998
61	WWII Pillbox 1942	80	Habitat Ardmore Park 1984–1986	99	Morley Road House 1998
62	Nassim Hill Apartments 1950–1951	81	Tampines North Community Centre 1989*	100	Camden Medical Centre 1999
63	Tiong Bahru Housing Estate 1936–1954	82	Singapore Indoor Stadium 1990	101	Coronation Road West House 1998–2000
64	Asia Insurance Building 1954	83	Hitachi Tower/Caltex House 1993	102	The Gallery Hotel 2000
65	Bank of China Building 1953–1954	84	Eu House I 1993–1994	103	Victoria Park Houses 2000
66	Blessed Sacrament Church 1961–1963	85	The Concourse 1994	104	Marine Parade Community Centre 2000
67	Peoples Park Complex 1970–1973	86	King Albert Park House 1992–1994	105	Expo MRT Station 2001*
68	Jurong Town Hall 1970*	87	Tampines New Town 1994*	106	Trevose Crescent 2002
69	Golden Mile Complex 1974	88	Wheelock Place 1994	107	The Esplanade – Theatres on the Bay 1994–2002
70	OCBC Tower 1975	89	UOB Plaza 1993–1995	108	Tree House 2002
71	Futura Apartments 1973–1976	90	Temasek Polytyechnic 1995*	109	1 Moulmein Rise 2003
72	Pearl Bank Apartments 1976	91	Eastpoint Shopping Centre 1996*	110	Lincoln Modern 2003
73	Singapore Power Building 1971–1977	92	Millenia Tower 1996	111	The Arris 2003
74	Pandan Valley Condominium 1973–1979	93	Check House I 1996	112	Villa O 2003*
75	Regent Hotel 1983	94	Genesis 1994–1997		* Not on maps

SINGAPORE ARCHITECTURE // 141

INDEX

A

Abrams, Charles 80
Akitek Tenggara 101, 106, 113, 124
Alsop, Will 109
Archigram Group 82, 94
Archiplan Team 100
Architects 61   45, 61, 75, 83, 102, 106, 110, 112, 116
Architects Team 3   23, 82, 91
Archurban Architects Planners   82, 95, 97
Archynamics Architects   82, 95
Arquitectonica 106

B

Bedmar and Shi   109, 111, 133
Bedmar, Ernesto   108, 111, 133
Bennett, John   11, 32, 36
BEP Akitek   82, 83, 93, 98
Beurel, Father Jean Marie   27
Bidwell RAJ   32, 37, 49, 51, 56
Booty and Edwards and Partners   80
Brewer, Frank   61, 70, 72
Brundle, KA   80, 84
Burgee, John   106, 119

C

Chalk, Warren   94
Chan Sau Yan   108, 122
Chan Soo Khian   108
Cheah Kok Ming   125
Chen Voon Fee   80
Cheng Heng Tat Associates   51
Chung and Wong   26, 42, 61
Church, AG   80
Coleman, George Drumgold   8, 9, 10, 11, 16, 19, 21, 27, 28, 29, 33, 36
Collyer, Colonel George   11
Combes, Louis Antoine   11
Cook, Peter   94
Cox, Philip   106
CPG Consultants Pte Ltd   35, 46, 56
Cruik, DM   37, 53
CSYA Architects   108, 109, 122
Cullinan, Edward   109

D

David Tay and Associates   66
Design Environment Group   47
Design International   58
Design Partnership   82, 89, 92, 99
Dowsett, Gordon   80, 88
DP Architects Pte Ltd   35, 42, 83, 99, 106, 109, 117, 119, 127, 134
Dyce, Charles Alexander   10, 27

E

Eisenman, Peter   127

F

Faber, CEF   10
Ferguson, William   37, 56
Ferrie, James and Partners   23, 80
FORUM Architects   35, 109
Foster and Partners   132
Foster, Norman   109, 132
Frazer, James Milner   60
Fry, Maxwell   84

G

Garnier, Tony   60
Gordon, A   60, 67, 77
Graves, Michael   127
Gropius, Walter   80
Grounds, Roy   80
Group 2 Architects   82, 96
Gwathmey, Charles   127

H

Hadid, Zaha   109
HAM Architects   109, 139
Hancock, THH   16
Hassell, Richard   109
Hedjuk, John   127
Herron, Ron   94
Hill, Kerry   108, 121
Ho Kwong Yew   61, 77
Housing and Development Board   81, 82, 83, 85, 114
Howard, Ebenezer   60
HYLA Architects   109

J

Jackson, Lieutenant Philip   9
James Stirling Michael Wilford and Associates   117
Johnson, Philip   106, 119

K

K2LD Architects   109
Kahn, Louis   80
Kay Ngee Tan   109, 120
Kepes, Gyorgy   80
Keys and Dowdeswell   60, 63, 65, 69
Keys, Major PH   63
KNTA Architects   120
Kobe, S   80
Koenisberger, OH   80
Koh Seow Chuan   89
Kohn Pederson Fox   109
Koren, Rolf   80
Kurokawa, Kisho   80, 83, 106, 109, 115

L

Le Corbusier   80, 81, 82, 92, 96, 137
Lee Sian Teck   47
Lim Chong Keat   80
Lim Ee Mun, Joseph   135
Lim, William   48, 80, 81, 82, 83, 89, 99, 104, 108, 109, 126, 129, 131
Ling Hao   139
Liu Thai Ker   82
LOOK Architects   109
Lothaire, Brother   11, 34
Lundon, Frank Gordon   60
Lutyens, Sir Edwin   37, 58, 72

M

MacLellan, P & W,   39, 48
McCallum, Major HE   36, 46
McNair, JFA   11, 35, 36, 38, 46
MacPherson, Colonel Ronald   11, 33
McRitchie, James   36, 37, 48
McSwiney, Dennis Lesley   10, 27
Maddock   19
Made Wijaya   125

Maekawa, Kunio 80, 82, 91
Maki, Fumihiko 82, 89, 109
Malayan Architects Co-Partnership 80, 82, 89
MAPS Design Studio 109
Mata, Soria y 82, 92
May, Ernst 60
Meadows, FD 60, 67, 77
Meier, Richard 109, 127
Mendelsohn, Erich 61, 77
Meng Ta Cheang 64
Metabolist Group 82, 89, 94
Michael, Brother 34
Middlemiss, CO 87
Mitchell Giurgola Thorp and Associates 106
MKPL Architects 109
Mok Wei Wei 109, 126, 138
Murphy Jahn 106, 110

N
Nain, Father RP Ch 11, 29, 34
Nash, John 8
Neumann, Alfred 82
Neutra, Richard 80
Ng Keng Siang 80, 86
Niemeyer, Oscar 80
Noli, Cavalieri Rodolfo 78, 87

O
OD Architects 64
Ong and Ong Architects Pte Ltd 29
Ong Chin Bee 82, 96
Oud, JP 60

P
Page, Lincoln 80
Palmer and Turner 80, 87
Pan-Malaysian Group Architects 47
Paris, Father Pierre 11
Pei, IM 82, 83, 93, 98, 102
Perrault, Dominic 106
Petrovitch, DS 61, 76
Poon Hin Kong 125

Portman, John 83, 98
Public Works Department 16, 32, 38, 39, 46, 71, 73, 75, 78, 84, 124, 125
Pugin, AWN 11
PWD Consultants 34, 57, 66, 80

Q
Quek Associates 48

R
Rae, DC 37, 56
RDC Architects Ptd Ltd 83, 103
Repellin, Didier 29, 35
Rietveld, GT 128
RMJM 109
Roche, Kevin and Dinkeloo, John 106, 119
RSP Architect, Planners and Engineers 44, 83, 105, 106, 115
Rudolph, Paul 81, 83, 100, 112

S
SAA Architects Pte Ltd 83
Saarinen, Eliel 61, 76
Safdie Moshe 82, 83, 103
Santry, Dennis 60, 65
SCDA Architects 108, 109, 128, 137
Seow Lee Heah and Partners 82, 94
Seow, Timothy 82, 94
Singapore Improvement Trust 60, 80, 85
Singapore Planning and Urban Research Group 82
Smithson, Peter and Alison 80, 82
Stanbury, Lt Col 37, 58
Stirling, James 106, 117
Stubbins, Hugh 83
Swan and Lermit 11
Swan and Maclaren 11, 29, 32, 37, 43, 45, 49, 51, 55, 57, 60, 61, 64, 65, 76

T
Tan Cheng Siong 82, 95, 97, 101
Tan Kok Meng 139
Tan Teck Khiam 109, 120
Tang Guan Bee 108, 118, 123, 129

Tange, Kenzo 83, 89, 106, 113, 124
Tangguanbee Architects 108, 109, 118, 123, 129
Tay Puay Huat 82, 96
Thomson, John Turnbull 10, 11, 26, 33
Tomlinson, Samuel 36, 37, 53
Tsao and McKown 106

U
Urban Renewal Authority 82, 83, 93, 98

V
Van der Rohe, Mies 80, 108, 137
Van Sitteran and Partners 80, 88

W
W Architects 109, 117, 134
Wakeman, POG 80
Ward, Frank Dorrington 60, 61, 71, 73, 75, 78
White, Michael 125
Wilford, Michael 109, 117, 134
WOHA Architects 109, 130, 136
Wong and Ouyang 106, 115
Wong Mun Summ 109
Wong, Alfred 80
Woolner, T 32

Y
Yong Kok Choo 59
Yorke, FRS 61, 84
Yeang, Ken 109

FOOTNOTES

1. Turnbull, C.M., *A History of Singapore 1819-1975*, Oxford University Press, 1977, p1. Also refererred to: Samuel, Dhoraisingam S., *Singapore's Heritage Through Places of Historical Interest*, Elixir, Singapore, 1991. p1
2. Turnbull, C.M., *A History of Singapore 1819–1975*, Oxford University Press, 1977, p2.
3. Hall, G D E, *A History of Southeast Asia*, London, 1965.
4. Hamilton, Alexander, *A New Account of the East Indies*, Vol II, Edinburgh, 1727, p52-53.
5. Turnbull, ibid. p5
6. Turnbull, ibid. p14
7. Drumgold sometimes appears as Drumgoolde.
8. Begbie, P. J. *The Malayan Peninsula*. London, 1834 p352, quoted in Seow Eu Jin, *Architectural Development in Singapore*, Unpublished PhD Thesis, University of Melbourne, 1974. p90.
9. Seow Eu Jin, *Architectural Development in Singapore*, Unpublished PhD Thesis, University of Melbourne, 1974.
10. Extracts from Raffles memo to Davis dated 4th November 1822 are recorded in Seow Eu Jin, ibid, p85
11. Tan, Lily (Editor), *Chinatown: an album of a Singapore community*, Times Books International, Singapore 1983.
12. Seow Eu Jin, ibid, p86
13. Seow Eu Jin, ibid, p157
14. Seow Eu Jin, ibid, p102.
15. Beamish, Jane and Jane Fergusson, *A History of Singapore Architecture*, Graham Brash, Singapore, 1985. p61
16. Frampton, Kenneth, *Modern Architecture: A Critical History*, Thames and Hudson, London, 1980. p42.
17. Seow Eu Jin, ibid, p202.
18. Lee, Kip Lin, *The Singapore House 1819-1942*, Times Editions, Singapore, 1988.
19. Edwards, Norman and Peter Keys, *Singapore: A Guide to Buildings, Streets, Places*, Times Books International, Singapore, 1988. p462
20. Beamish, Jane and Jane Fergusson, *A History of Singapore Architecture*, Graham Brash, Singapore, 1985.
21. Seow, Eu Jin, ibid, p397.
22. Choe, Alan F C, *Objectives in Urban Renewal*, First Congress of the Singapore National Academy of Science, Singapore, 14th August 1968.
23. Powell, Robert, 'Inciting Rebellion', in *No Limits: Articulating William Lim*, Select Books, Singapore, 2002. p20
24. Powell, Robert, 'Inciting Rebellion', in *No Limits: Articulating William Lim*, Select Books, Singapore, 2002. p22
25. Powell, Robert, A Process of (Un)learning, in *Modern Tropical Architecture: Tay Kheng Soon and Akitek Tenggara*, Page 1, Singapore, 1997, p 16.
26. Powell. Robert, 'Inciting Rebellion', in *No Limits: Articulating William Lim*, Select Books, Singapore, 2002. p16.
27. Edwards, Norman and Peter Keys, *Singapore: A Guide to Buildings, Streets, Places*, Times Books International, Singapore, 1988.
28. Lim, William SW, "A Tale of the Unexpected", Special Commonwealth Association of Architects Session, International Union of Architects (UIA) Congress, Brighton, UK, 13-17th July, 1987.
29. Tay Kheng Soon, "A World Class City deserves a World Class Architecture", Conference on *Towards Excellence in the Built Environment*, Singapore, 3-4 December, 1987. p2
30. Tay Kheng Soon, "A World Class City deserves a World Class Architecture", Conference on *Towards Excellence in the Built Environment*, Singapore, 3-4 December, 1987.
31. Powell, Robert, *Singapore: Architecture of a Global City*, Archipeligo Press. Edition Didier Millet, Singapore, 2000. p12
32. Powell, Robert, *Modern Tropical Architecture: Tay Kheng Soon and Akitek Tenggara*, Page 1, Singapore, 1997. p163
33. Lee Kip Lin *Telok Ayer Market* (1983), *Emerald Hill* (1984) and *The Singapore House* (1989).
34. Liu, Gretchen. *Pastel Portraits: Singapore's Architectural Heritage*, Singapore Cordinating Committee, Select Books Singapore, 1984.
35. Lim, Vincent, "Nothing but More", *d+a*, 014/2003, Singapore, June 2003. p21